SNIPPETS

SNIPPETS

Invitation to
Celebrate Life
New Orleans Style

A.V. Margavio

ARPress
ILLUMINATING IDEAS.
EMPOWERING VOICES

ARPress
45 Dan Road Suite 5
Canton MA 02021

Hotline: 1(888) 821-0229
Fax: 1(508) 545-7580

Ordering Information:

Quantity sales. Special discounts are available on quantity purchases by corporations, associations, and others. For details, contact the publisher at the address above.

Printed in the United States of America.

ISBN-13:   Softcover   979-8-89330-149-6
                eBook   979-8-89330-150-2

Library of Congress Control Number: 2024902495

CONTENTS

ACKNOWLEDGEMENTS

I wish to acknowledge my family for their faithfulness and good cheer as I buried myself in my work. Would that I could list them by name, but the publisher insisted this not exceed the length of "War and Peace". Still, I need to thank number one son, Vic, for all his computer magic. Also, I would like to thank my wife, Sandy, for not having me committed. Thanks go to David Moreland for the alligator photo and the gator for his kindness during the photo shoot. Kudos go to Loyd Abadie and Robert for finding and correcting rogue words and sentences in the tangle of text. Special thanks goes to Kait Margavio for her patient editting. To all the family, this is for you. So, Smile. Readers should be pleased that I persuaded my granddauther, Olivia Margavio, to come out of retirement to create delightful sketches for their pleasure.

INTRODUCTION

Y ou always wanted to write your memoirs, but never could find the time. Don't fret, I will write it for you. How is this possible? I am glad you asked. Have you ever sat around with friends and someone felt compelled, for reasons only known to God, to tell a tale that seduces others to try to top it? "My Aunt Bertha fell asleep while watching tv and my cousin Bill placed eleven empty bottles of beer in her lap, just in time for Uncle Frank to see and assume the worst"! Once out there, the first tale induces others to "tell all". The accounts can be funny, sad. grave, in good or bad taste, but always beckon others to share memories. Therefore, I write this little book to summon the reader's memories from the forgotten snippets buried by a busy life overconcerned with time management.

The graying of the West has not slowed the pace of modern life. With increasing numbers of the elderly, one would think that the pace would shift into lower gear, but that hasn't happened. In fact, the tempo of life appears to have accelerated. Much of our time is spent being very busy. We hurry and wait and hurry and wait. The waiting hasn't gotten longer; we have become more impatient with and less tolerant of life's many delays.

I cite as partial evidence of my claim the rise of the fast-food industry. That development has left us more intolerant of delays. How else can we explain the oft mentioned jibe at a fast-food establishment that it serves a new category of food, "slow-fast food"?

In contemporary times, time itself has become a much sort after commodity, a highly prized object that one can purchase at the shopping mall and super market, provided that one doesn't get stuck in traffic.

But we also dread time for the devastation that it brings to our bodies and to our possessions. There are a number of new industries that have sprung up whose aim it is to stay the ravages of time. Cosmetic surgery immediately comes to mind. Therefore, we guard the double gates of time simultaneously coaxing it to speed up and slow down. Ironically, we waste a good bit of time starring at clocks or asking others for the time.

To remedy this awful state of affairs, I offer "snippets" for those too busy to read as well as those who find themselves in frequent traffic jams. One can read a "snippet" in the time it takes to order a burger. At a "slow-fast food" establishment, one may even be able to read a half dozen or more. Only God knows how many can be read in a traffic jam. And if, here and there, you find amusement reading a "snippet", remember that laughter is known to be the best remedy for slowing the rudeness of time.

A "snippet" is a really short story not unlike the explanation necessary to communicate a play on words joke. Its intention is to summon into memory a moment, an episode in life. While one can argue for a complete story full of developed characters, a plot, climax, and conclusion, I fancy that life isn't that way. I do believe that life has a purpose and is soaked in meaning, but the essential meaning is embedded in the endless parade of largely unconnected moments, in the eternal now. "Now is the day of salvation" declares the psalmist. "This is the day the Lord has made; let us rejoice and be glad"- I might add, there is no other. But the human mind was made to find order and meaning and even unconnected events must have some minimal organization.

I organize my memories chronologically and spatially and so does the human race. Who a person relates to changes as one passes from childhood to adolescence to adulthood and then to retiree. Each season of life has a unique set of relationships and our memories are embedded in the relationships that are party to their creation. Thus, each section of the book records the memories of a particular time frame and a specific set of relationships. Each individual encounters some, if not all, of the changes that come with life's seasons, friends and family in childhood, peers in adolescence, spouse and children in adulthood; colleagues at work; and grandchildren in retirement. In a real sense "snippets' are universal memories, events that not only have happened in the past, but will continue to happen. And the reader is invited to tarry a spell down memory lane. But memories are embedded in space, in a particular locality and with a singular ambiance. I give the time and place at the end to give much more necessary detail.

A Bad Boy and the Rooster's Revenge

The large two-story house in the middle of the 8300 block of Apple Street was one of the first homes in the area. According to family memory, it was originally built around 1900 by my grandfather, Mateo Costanza. In the nineteenth century, the area was on the outskirts of the old town of Carrolton, a small semi-rural village upriver from the fashionable Garden District.

It's hard to imagine today, but New Orleans in the middle of the twentieth century was still largely a constellation of villages that today are called neighborhoods. It was not unusual for New Orleanians to raise chickens, provided they had the space. Fresh eggs and fried chicken on Sunday were the payoff for the families that had the space, will and stomach to keep chickens. My mother would select a chicken on Saturday and wring its neck. She assured me that her technique was the most humane way to dispatch the poor bird. In hindsight, she seemed reluctant and almost apologetic, whether for her benefit or mine, I do not know. But unapologetically, she handed me the bird for plucking. I would place it in a bucket of warm water and begin to remove its feathers. To this day, the smell of chicken fat returns to memory that foul task.

It was sometime during my early childhood that our family abandoned chicken raising. And the chicken shed and yard became part of my playing field, but not before the following unhappy incident.

As a very young child, I would frequently relieve myself whenever I found myself too busy to go inside. The proximity of chickens presents an intoxicating temptation and challenge to a young boy. For me it soon became a bad habit. The thought of baptizing as many chickens as possible became a game of skill. I was particularly fond of wetting the mean rooster. In my own defense, I should argue that the practice is more of a sport than what some little boys do with sticks. Nonetheless, I persisted in my perverse habit for some time until my quickness in backing away from the fence separating the rooster and me was slower than the rooster's advance. On that painful day, my tears would evoke only suppressed laughter and a stern reprimand from my mother.

Now the lesson that I learned that day is that all God's creatures deserve respect and when we fail to give it, they will sometimes extract it from us. And I candidly confess that there were many more times that I gave God's creatures due cause to exact revenge. I remember the time that… but that's a snippet for another day.

First Grade Lovers

When I was in the first grade, my next-door neighbor and fellow first grader, John, hatched a sinister plot. I am sure, if asked, he would claim that it was I and not he that initiated that criminal conspiracy. But I am equally certain that it was he and not I that did so. Whatever confusion surrounding the authorship of the dastardly collusion may be, the scheme itself is crystal clear. The gist of our felonious plan was to hide in wake to pounce upon a beautiful blue-eyed blond, who had only recently enrolled in our school. Taking advantage of the element of surprise, we intended to kiss her. With diabolic coordination, we hid behind a bush, aided by the element of surprise, we kissed her. Knocking her down in the process, she immediately began to cry. Her fair complexion evaporated. In its place fear and shame turned her once angelic face devil red. I vaguely remember that after carrying out our predatory intent, we entered the school grounds as if nothing happened, but not before we helped her up and brushed off the dust. We were always high-minded gentlemen.

The tortured reasoning of adult felons often perplexes criminologists, but the mind of a first grader is an inscrutable unexplored wilderness. And for this reason, I can offer no illumination. I don't recall any discussion between John and me as to how we would explain our actions. Suffice it to say that adult criminals usually have exit strategies or alibis. We, however, gave no thought to what might happen when our victim reported the crime. Perhaps, we thought she would be amused by the affair and find it enjoyable. She was not.

The very next memory I have of the incident is standing before our principal, a large Irish nun. "Antony", she said with mock sternness.

She always pronounced my name without the "th" sound. "Antony, what did you do"? As I remember it, her voice and demeanor did not betoken anger. I fancy that she fought back the laughter. Although, in all honesty I must say I was terrified. After all, she was a very large nun and I was a very bad but little boy. And I just wanted to go home to my mama.

I often wondered what would happen to first grade lovers if they were caught today. Do you suppose they would be judicated as sex offenders and their photos distributed by the Post Office?

Grade School

It is said that kindergarten is academic boot camp. We didn't have kindergarten. I started school in the first grade and graduated in the eighth grade at Incarnate Word. We had two recess periods and an hour for lunch recess. If we still had the wiggles in class, the teacher would stop whatever we were doing and direct us in calisthenics. It was always fun and amusing to watch our teacher, in full habit, jump up and down. With their radar operational, the nuns could detect whether the whole class needed exercise or just one kid. Typically, it was a boy with a wiggle problem.

The potential behavior problem was sent on errands. "Take this note to First Grade". Or, "Take this chalk to Fourth Grade". And off you went, up and down the stairs. Sometimes, the errand was to clean the chalk erasers. I loved to do that. You would get to bang a half dozen erasers against the basketball goal post. This is what teachers did before the developments of meds for attention deficit and hyperactivity.

I never could understand the claim that Catholic schools regimented children. Incarnate Word's lunch period was a full hour and kids were allowed to go home for lunch, bring lunch, or eat in the cafeteria. It is true, the nuns would carefully check the older boys for the tell-tale signs of smoking. Perhaps my recollections are clouded by fond memories and I just don't recall the problems some complain about today.

On most days, unless inclement weather prevented it, the whole school from first grade to eighth grade assembled on the school grounds after Mother Superior rang the bell. After a drum roll and a cymbal clash, National Anthem was played. In orderly fashion, each grade walked to their respective classroom. Teaching began after prayers and roll call.

Morning assembly was particularly memorable for me because I was responsible for the drum roll. I alone played the drum roll that preceded the cymbal clash that was followed by the Anthem. For a brief moment all eyes were on me. I awaited the bandmaster's cue to initiate the roll and I made that drum sing with no small amount of gusto. It was a source of pride to realize that school couldn't start without me! When things went smoothly, it was an impressive performance. But things didn't always go well.

To this very day, I have not mastered time. I usually am way too early or marginally late. On more than one occasion, I remember Mother Superior, a tall Irish woman and bigger than life, shout out. "Hurry" Antony"! "You're going to be late for your own funeral". But, when I straightened my drum strap, I gave the best drum roll a person with two left hands could give. Then came the clash of cymbals and the patriotic sounds filled the whole school yard and flowed out into the surrounding streets. How could a person not feel pride? Neither nature nor personal habits of punctuality prepared me for the role I played.

Old Ones

I suppose most families experienced an inconvenient visit at dinner time. It can be a bit uncomfortable, particularly when the guests refuse to eat. My recollection, however, is that two relatives in particular always made their appearance just as my mother was setting the table. It happened so regularly that the uncomfortableness was swallowed up by familiarity, and annoyance was wiped away by the hand of amusement. They made us laugh.

Our great aunt and uncle, Barina and Liborio lived only about four blocks away and walked to our house. They were a mismatched pair. She was tall and stout and he was short and lean. She lumbered and he trotted, impatient to reach his destination. A half of a city block separated them as they made their way to our house. And the separation between them was intolerable for my great uncle, he would stop and shout, "affretarsi". She always replied, but I was always too far away to hear her response. To be sure, it was an insult, judging by the hand gestures that accompanied it. At the sight of them, I knew that I could expect a piece of gum.

Unfortunately, the piece of gum was not a whole stick. She would reach in a purse and retrieve a single stick of doublemint gum. She would tear the stick into as many pieces as there were children present. In broken English she would say, "A piece-a for you, a piece-a for you". She could sometimes get four pieces from a single stick. It was just enough to taste and not ruin your dinner.

At dinner, great uncle would man his chair at table, not to eat, but to be our cheer leader. In his younger days, he was a big eater. He developed a digestion problem in old age, but that did not keep him from enjoying the appetite of others. I would eat like a wolf and so would my brothers. "Ah! You liki . Eat it!". All through the meal, he would cheer our appetites on. He brought the same dramatic element to watching TV with us.

When we watched cowboy shows on TV, he became a one-man chorus in a Greek play. In the 1950s, it was easy to know which cowboy to root for. "Ya, you gottum. Shoot'um"! He never sat still, but would jump up and down as he shouted out warnings to the cowboys wearing white hats. He was more dramatic than the shoot'um up scene.

What to cook. what to cook. what to cook?

Italian Lessons

Our home on Apple St. was originally built by my maternal grandfather. Mateo was a short barrel-chested immigrant from the Sicilian village of Alia. He was already an old man when I was a child. He resided in New Orleans ever since he arrived in the United States at the age of seventeen.

I fondly remember him playing his guitar and singing arias. What really stands out in my memory was singing his prayers in Latin with the accompaniment of his guitar. The solemn sounds would fill both stories of the old house and flowed into the street. He was proud to claim the status, acolyte. And he sang his prayers with gusto. "Santo Paola… ora pro nobis. Santa Maria… ora pro nobis".

There were times he would sit on the front porch swing and strum his guitar to a Sicilian ditty. Near as I can tell the neighbors didn't mind. But once, a neighbor expressed her condolence to my mother. Evidently, she thought he was senile. "I am really sorry about your father", she said. My mother assured the neighbor that there was nothing wrong with my grandfather. My grandfather would not have understood this expression of concern. "A happy heart sings", he would say.

From time to time he would call my friend and I into his room to "ballare e cantara". Instinctively we would jump up and down (dance) and mimic his words (sing) and laugh. But the dancing and singing was always preceded by Italian language lessons. He often reminded my mother to teach us Italian. Her reply was that the children learn English in school. His counter argument was, "They can learn English in the streets, but where would they learn Italian"?

Lessons would begin with the vowel sounds and then the names of body parts. He would point to his head and say, testa. And then, occhi, bocca, orecchio, capelli, as he pointed to his eyes, mouth, ear, and hair. And he would also teach us to count in Italian. Uno, due, tre, quattro, etc.

At the end of each lesson, he would strum an appropriate chord and shout out, "ballare e cantara"! We would laugh and then he would laugh. When we all had a good laugh, he would set his guitar aside and reach inside his trousers for his draw string purse and retrieve as many nickels as there were dancers. "Uno picayune for you and uno picayune for you" with a heavy emphasis on the second to last vowel. A picayune in New Orleans is a nickel.

When he was old and no longer could tend his vegetable garden, he would pay us a penny for each bucket of water we carried to the backyard. And when he was "full of days", and at the ripe age of 97, he died. He didn't pass away, he died. I can see him with my mind's eye strumming his guitar, singing and dancing before God. "Sanctus, Sanctus, Sanctus".

The Shoe Shop

My father's shoe shop was something of a neighborhood landmark. The neighborhood itself was rather typical of New Orleans working class neighborhoods. As Fontainebleau Avenue crosses South Carrolton Avenue, the name changes to Apple Street and suddenly, stately residences replaces unpretentious doubles.

From its beginning, Apple Street had always been a mixture of private residences and businesses. In the 1940s and 1950s, nearly every block had at least one tavern. My father's shoe shop was in the middle of the 8300 block, which had a tavern on each corner. The half dozen blocks that stretched from Carrolton Avenue to Leonidas Street could boast of having a Chinese laundry, several grocery stores, a drug store, hardware store, a sweet shop, a movie theater, and an assortment of other businesses. And two blocks from the shoe shop was Incarnate Word Church and School.

In many ways, the neighborhood was a village somewhat insulated from outside influences. It was as parochial as a country town. But this could be said of most American cities at that time, outside of a handful of truly cosmopolitan centers. The only significant breech of its walls was radio and the movies, and generally these media reinforced local traditions, and when they didn't, they were ignored. Television was in its infancy and broadcasts were too infrequent to challenge values. Of course, the late 1950s and 1960s brought significant changes, but that's another story.

Looking back on it, the shoe shop was an ideal place to watch the drama of life unfold. Every Saturday and sometimes during the week in the late afternoons, I was the shoeshine boy, a task that allowed me to make some money. More importantly, it was the stage on which I could glimpse life's dramatic moments.

Readers born after 1970 will find the way social and economic elements were still interwoven in the 1950s puzzling. But visiting any store was as much a social event as it was an economic necessity. You got more than food at a grocery and more than shoes repaired at the shoe shop. You exchanged gossip, renewed friendships, and enjoyed the encounters. It was not uncommon for customers to wait for their shoes to be fixed. And then, of course, they returned as wear on their soles necessitated or the desire to socialize was awakened. Thus, the shoe shop provided a box seat from which I could view princes and paupers, rogues and saints. Stories of tragedy and comedy were retold amidst the leather dust and loud machinery of the shoe shop.

One of the more memorable comic actors on stage was a young man in his late twenties or early thirties. My eldest brother called him "Crazy Tony" and said that he could make a dead man laugh. He certainly could make us laugh and he did it without trying. In the idiom of today, you could say that he was "off the wall".

One day, Crazy Tony came in the shop and decided to wait for his shoes to be resoled. He engaged my eldest brother in light conversation. I could tell from my brother's face that Tony was in full character. I drew close to hear over the noisy machinery. It did not take long for my father to pause and listen. And the story we were told was in perfect harmony with Tony's persona.

We all knew that Tony loved to eat and cook. He had been going on and on about how good his roast duck had been. What we did not know, but only suspected, were the lengths that he would go to get a good meal. But we found out when my brother asked where he got the roasted duck. Tony proceeded to detail his technique. He buys a loaf of bread and drives to Audubon Park. He opens the backdoor of his Chevy sedan. He feeds the ducks long enough to gain their trust. He directs a trail of breadcrumbs toward the opened door. Finally, when a gaggle of ducks is in full feeding frenzy, he chases them into the Chevy. A quick door slam and a fast get away seals the fate of the hapless ducks.

Now the real advantage of watching life from the shoe shop is that you can usually count on a sequel to a story. Later that same year, a friend of "Crazy Tony" was in the shop and it was from him that we heard that Tony had been arrested in Audubon Park. Not for stealing ducks, but for trying to procure venison at the Zoo. I don't recall the outcome, nor do I recall the precise details of his plan to get a deer. But I am sure that his deer plan was as brilliant as his duck plan.

"Grandmaw" comes for Breakfast

Walker Percy insisted that New Orleans is a different kind of place. When I first read "New Orleans Mon Amour", I accepted his thesis without much critical hesitation. However, it wasn't until I recalled some personal episodes and quaint curiosities reported by others did I really see some of the implications of his view.

New Orleans is a place of contrasts, naked women and nuns, revelry of Mardi Gras and the solemnity of lent. rich and poor and black and white. Where else in the world would the Pope be roundly greeted with that familiar New Orleans welcome afforded close friends, "Where yat Pope"?

I first saw the larger community from the parochial portal of my father's shoe repair shop. My childhood memories are filled with the amazing cast of characters that made their entrance in on pilgrimage, like the characters one encounter's in Chaucer's tales. Now Grandmaw was but one member of the cast of characters that made New Orleans so memorable for me, a persona at once bewildering to non-natives and so familiar to natives that she hardly seems worth mentioning.

"Grandmaw" was an old Black woman in ill-fitting old clothes with a kerchief fastened over her head as a makeshift hat. She was small and thin; one would be tempted to say frail were it not for her august spirit. At times she sported a corncob pipe firmly planted in her toothless mouth. From time to time she would pay a visit to the shoe shop and ask for money and shoes. I never saw my father refuse anyone money, free shoes long abandoned by their original owners, or a reduction in price for repair. My mother's charity was also freely extended. Both parents played out their roles of charity from a familiar New Orleans script. When "Grandmaw" finished collecting from father, she would make her way to the back of our house by way of an alley and boldly knock on the kitchen door. "Rosie, I come for my breakfast", she demanded. "Okay, I'll bring it in a minute". My mother was somewhat irritated by the interruption. When mother gathered the fixings for "Grandmaw's" breakfast, she would serve her on the stoop (most houses were raised on brick pillars). From time to time, "Grandmaw" would ask for seconds. "Rosie, give me some mo of that sweet coffee". Mother was clearly relieved when "Grandmaw" departed and strangely would show concern when "Grandmaw" tarried too long before her next visit.

It is understandable that any mention of kindness to Blacks in the old South evokes the charge of paternalism, that deep-rooted defense with which many southerners hid their prejudices from themselves. But "Grandmaw" was no Aunt Jemima and the good old darky role was not in her script. In some ways, she anticipated present day philanthropists who demand contributions and ply hefty ones from their intimidated donors. The fact is that New Orleans scarcely lost its old-world roots and its institutionalized alms giving. If truth were told, the whole affair stems from the fact that in New Orleans, a tradition can arise from almost anything, including a knock at the door. An act once or twice repeated becomes carved in stone, consecrated and another tradition is born.

A case in point involved the Little Sisters of the Poor who would made their rounds, usually as a twosome, to local businesses collecting for the poor. Once I was told that a patron of an upscale restaurant in the French Quarter was scandalized when he noticed two nuns seated dinning on rich fare. He inquired from the waiter the meaning of this hypocrisy and insult to justice. The waiter reassured the agitated patron that the little sisters had not forsaken their vow of holy poverty for they were dinning on the house, a long-standing practice of the restaurant. The patron, still unsatisfied awaited a fuller explanation. "You see Sir, the little nuns would go to the kitchen at the rear of the restaurant to collect money for the poor. Well, one day the cook asked the nuns if they would like to try a new dish and wanted their opinion on the matter. The cook brought a couple of chairs for the sisters. Someone remarked that the nuns must be very uncomfortable seated in a hot kitchen in full black habit. Somebody else suggested that it would be more pleasant for the little nuns to dine in the air-conditioned dining area. So, when the Little Sisters of the Poor show up at the kitchen door, they are escorted to "their" table in the dining room". Thus, tradition is borne and reason is mocked.

All Alone

Our old house on Apple Street was large enough to include two upstairs apartments and a small one downstairs. As a child, I remember a family of three renting for over a decade. They became a familiar presence in our kitchen. But by the 1960s, renters were mostly individuals, or as in one case, a young mother with an eight-year-old boy. Typically, occupancy was brief, and I have no enduring recollections of most, but the mother with a young boy still weighs heavily in my memory. The incident I recall occurred when I returned home from a date.

I was a bit of a night owl. My date and I went to a concert and then to Cafe Du Monde in the Quarter for coffee and donuts. As I drove my 1952 Ford in the driveway, I suddenly was more awake than I cared to be. A little boy was sitting on the bottom step of the stairs that led to his apartment. I hastened to turn off the car lights which were shining in his eyes. I made my way to him as he sat up and walked towards me. I asked him why he was up so late. What he told me was something that my naive brain could not fathom. He awoke and discovered that his mother was not home, but he couldn't tell me how long he was alone. I realized that I had to stay with him until his mother returned and try to dispel his fears. I don't remember how long we talked, but I won't forget the question he posed to himself in my presence, "Every time I fall to sleep, you think she leaves?" The question disturbed me and lingered long in my thoughts like an after taste of bitterness.

It wasn't long after that episode that this mother and child left our house on Apple Street. I don't recall asking for or receiving an explanation. Since it was mother's role to rent the apartments, it would fall to her to speak to renters when problems arose. She gave me no explanation that I recall. What, if anything, my mother told her, I don't know. I do know what she would not do. She would not abandon them to the streets. "No room in the inn for a mother and child."; no! She would not and could not do that!

Toys Kids Made

Yes, there was a time when kids made toys. If you got skates for Christmas, you didn't throw them away when they were worn and broken, you resourced them. The front and back wheels were easily separated. Attached to 2 X 4s, they were turned into a skate mobile. The front 2 X 4 pivoted and the rider's feet steered, assisted by a rope held in hand. Pushed by a buddy, it was a side walk thrill when crashing through empty metal garbage cans. If only one skate was available, front and rear wheels were attached to respective ends of a 2 X 4. A vertical member was added to what became the front, to which a handle was attached. Your scooter was ready for riding, after it was properly decorated with bottle caps on the vertical member.

Centered around transportation, racing and thrill seeking, skate mobiles and scooters were guy things. I think girls took better care of their skates and, therefore, there were no broken skates to repurpose. Whether or not that guess is correct, girls took better care of their skates. Generally, skaters wore their skate key around their necks in necklace fashion. Skate "keys" were used to fasten and unfasten skates to one's shoes, that constantly needed retightening.

Happy the kid who could combine skating and chores. Having to run an errand didn't stop play, it accomplished the chore faster. Work that took longer could be paired with skating to make the chore less onerous. My mother, being the only girl in her family, was expected to iron shirts for six brothers and her father. Irons were heated in the fireplace prior to WWI. As the iron lost heat, it would be returned to the fireplace. You needed at least two irons for uninterrupted ironing. My mother's strategy was to iron a shirt, replace the iron and descend the stairs. Once downstairs, she would put on her skates and skate around the block. She would repeat these steps until her ironing duties were completed. But what do you do when even the wheels are unusable? You make other toys with whatever is available.

From apple crates, discarded inner tubes and spring clothes pins, rubber gun pistols were made. From old mops and broom handles, rifles were made. For a cannon, nothing is better than a wooden saw horse over which a bicycle tube was stretched. It took at least two strong kids to load and discharge it. And to what purpose were these instruments of pain put? War! War games were organized and strategized. The army picked by lot to defend the fort (club house) was always given the cannon. Boys played soldier roles until manhood swept them up to fight in a foreign land far away from clubhouse and home.

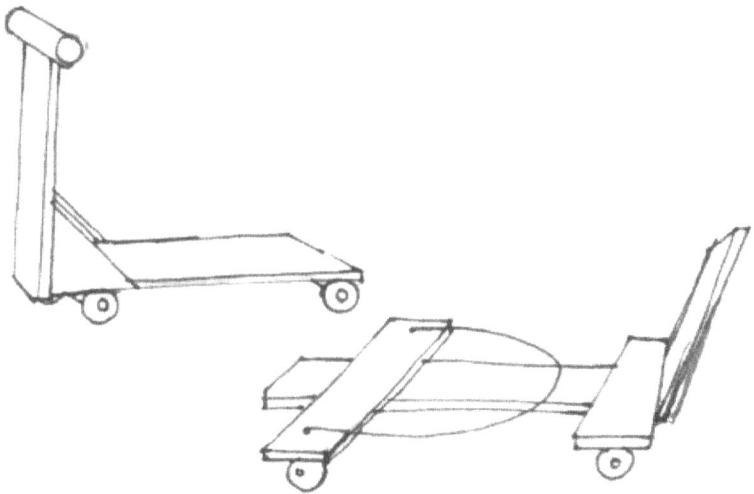

Levees and Sleds

South Louisiana is as flat as a fritter, except for levees and Monkey Hill. As far as I know, Monkey Hill is the highest peak in the New Orleans area. It's a product of civil engineering raised so that children in the flat world could see what a hill looks like, to climb up and down or seek the thrill of a very fast bicycle descent. Without hills or snow, how do children experience the thrill of a sled ride? Levees are everywhere in South Louisiana. The theory is that they keep water at bay. This is true, but they are also used as an endless green space to stroll atop and welcome summer breezes that rise in the evening.

Levees flank the River, the southern shore of Lake Pontchartrain and most other waterways. While levees are great for family strolls to escape the summer heat, kids love them for the speed of descent on any wheeled contraption at their disposal. When toy vendors invented "Big Wheels", their wedding to levees was predictable.

Who would have thought older kids would find fun on a tricycle? But walk it up a levee and take your feet off the petals, and you fly down at crash speed. "Big Wheels" were not around when I was a kid. I do confess that I tried my children's once or twice, though; the frame is much too small for a grown up or big kid. As a kid, I had to get my thrills on the steep levee slopes through other means. Any dummy can ride a snow sled, but it takes a rocket scientist to master a cardboard sled.

When the spell of summer is over and the sticky air is replaced by cool dry breezes from the north, hope is rising. But first, the levee must be covered with dry leaves, "New Orleans snow". Since "snow" doesn't always pile up where you want it to, you must gather the dry leaves and cascade them down the levee from top to bottom. With a piece of cardboard placed atop the levee, you runup the levee from the opposite side and plant both feet squarely on the sled. Get ready for a thrill or a big disappointment. If the leaves are damp or too sparse to reduce drag, you descend about six feet at walking speed. But when the static electricity is cracking, you are sledding! To what can I compare the experience? It is not an adrenaline rush. Nor is it a dangerous activity. Have you ever seen a bear or dog scratch its back on a tree? Have you seen lizards sun bathing or dogs running at full speed to jump in a pond? It's a burst of joy for life, like a family of deer suddenly reaching top speed for the fun of it. It's a thanksgiving for life. Alright, maybe that is a bit over dramatic. But not by much.

Bard of the Neighborhood

No matter how small the community, somewhere in it there is a person who is gifted with half of the prophetic spirit. They don't have the ability to see the future, but can "see" a deeper meaning in present things than others. This ability is not a product of book learning or professional experience, it is a gift that can't be bought or sold. It challenges the hearer to "see" beyond the words. Perhaps, an example will clarify my meaning. To a person who falsely claims American Indian ancestry, a bard would call them "fauxchahondas". This moniker could only be used of a female whose claim was rather thin. Bards have no particular status in the community apart from "bardness". They can be your next-door neighbor or the President of the United States. Monikers that they invent allow others to "see" individuals and events with uncanny sharpness. I urge the reader to recollect anyone they encountered who fits this description. The following examples may help retrieve a long-forgotten bard.

A neighbor of the Shoe Shop was gifted with "bardness". He propagated a moniker for a middle-aged couple who both wore bathing suits when outside. It was not anything that offended neighborhood standards, except that it was a bit unusual. He once referred to them as Adam and Eve. It stuck like glue. Not only was it an appropriate name for a semi-clad couple, but because it also captured their relationship. They were always together all alone in their Garden of Eden.. Perhaps, another example will recover a loss memory.

There was a middle-aged woman who frequented the Shoe Shop, whose appearance prompted an appropriate moniker. She had wiry gray untamed hair that sprang loose from her head on one side and gave the impression of one turning left while running in a strong wind.

Her movements were jerky and squirrel like. She spoke in short choppy sentences and her ideas were impossible to follow. The bard called her "the spirit". Less the reader thinks that the bard is one who is unkind and callous, let me suggest that reality is neither kind nor mean; it simply is. Later in life I would encounter other communities and other bards.

As a young unmarried single, I encountered a totally different "neighborhood". A popular young woman in our group had some kind of neurological condition that manifested itself in a continuous bobbing up and down motion. Nobody inquired why, she was just the "chicken". When I was introduced to her, I thought that the nickname was cruel. As I settled into my new relationships, I realized that the moniker shifted attention away from the condition toward the person. Paradoxically, it accomplished this by calling attention to it. In effect, it routinized it until it became ordinary and forgettable. Most nicknames, however, lack "bardness", like the one given to me.

A childhood bout with polio left me with a partially paralyzed right eye lid. I became "Popeye", a name that lacked inspiration. It wasn't until I smoked a pipe did the nickname sound reasonable. But it died on the vine and never pointed to anything more than a superficial appearance.

A Hobo Comes to Visit

All sorts of interesting people would come to Margavio's Shoe Repair Shop. Priests and nuns would come from neighboring parishes and have their shoes repaired for the price of the materials. Policeman would come to get boots or holsters repaired. If one needed corrective shoes, my father could modify shoes according to physicians' specification. And the shoeless could find a free pair of forgotten unclaimed shoes.

I believe I was in my early teens when a hobo came for shoes. Hobos are homeless by choice. Today, many are without homes due to dire economic circumstances, drug addiction, mental illness and for other reasons live on the streets. It's hard to imagine someone making homelessness a life style choice, but it was common during the early twentieth century. Our visitor chose homelessness and was not ashamed to admit it. On the contrary, he came puffing his life style.

His Italian ancestry served him well as he full throated sang the praises of freedom from the noisome rules of society. "I don't tell anyone where I am going or why", he pushed his ideology of freedom. "If I don't want to shave or bathe, why should I"? This line resonated with me. By the time he described the freedom and fun of riding freight trains, I was a believer. My father was amused as he handed him a pair of unclaimed shoes and a few coins to keep the jingle in his pocket. Off he went to breathe the air of freedom along the rails and in cattle cars.

I never forgot the "praise of freedom" and when a friend of mine tried to recruit me to leave home, I remembered all that hobo wisdom. I came close to leaving, but by the time we made preparations, it was getting dark. I heard the train sound its warning as it crossed Jefferson

Ave. Train whistles sound so lonely, especially at night. And then there was the smell of supper. Songs of freedom were tempting, but meat balls and pasta in a thick tomato sauce were more tempting. And just maybe we might have homemade donuts or tapioca with maraschino cherries.

Uncle Philip Comes to Visit

Everyone has an uncle who is special in some way. Special can mean almost anything. It could mean that the uncle is a lunatic or a WWII hero. My Uncle Philip was blinded from an accident when he was nineteen. Flying debris from hammering struck one eye. In those days, early 20th century, much less could be done for him. Eventually, he lost sight in both eyes. He supported himself, his wife and her child from a previous marriage by selling mops and brooms door to door.

I always admired him for his courage and ability. To maneuver mops and brooms onto street cars and buses, make change and all the other difficulties he faced from day to day, required heroic virtue. Yes, from time to time, a customer would pay with slugs. I don't think much bothered him. He always had a sense of humor and a willingness to help others.

When I was an infant, he would put me on his lap, until mother returned. Sometimes, she would go downtown to order supplies for the shoe shop. He remained sitting with me on his lap until mother returned. He would be wet, but never complained. My mother's "thank you" was augmented by cooking him his favorite meal. Whenever she planned on cooking red beans and rice, she would call Uncle Philip. She was conflicted because the dish required a good deal of salt, an ingredient hypertension sufferer, as he was, should not eat.

I watched him clean his plate without missing a bean or grain of rice. With hands over the plate, he could detect heat rising and knew exactly when to commence and when to wait for the signal for seconds. Nobody could enjoy red beans and rice more. I would watch him carefully to see if he missed or dropped and food. He never did. It was always a happy occasion when he came to visit except when I received a toy train one Christmas.

I laid out the tracks in a terrible place and it was necessary for the family to watch their steps. For a blind person, it was impossible to enter the room without stepping on tracks. And as fate would have it, his foot bore down on the layout. When I saw the damage, I looked at my mother. Her eyes said, "If ever there was a time for you not to throw a temper tantrum, now is that time". I picked up the broken tracks and looked up, but didn't say a word. Graciously, I thanked him for the toys he brought to me and my brothers. Of course, I complained about the ruined railroad track after he left, I was a spoiled brat.

Jack's Back

Everyone has had or knows someone who has or had a pet that acted more like a member of the family than a household pet. Jack, a young collie, came to our house one day from nowhere. My sister fell in love with him and so did the whole family. Jack liked to roam, but didn't go far.

The family became attached to Jack, so attached, that it was a big disappointment when we discovered that Jack wasn't our dog. His real owner lived just two blocks away. My sister's heart sunk when she realized Jack did not belong to her. And, indeed, our family was crestfallen. The only consolation the family experienced was due to the realization that Jack was a mere two blocks away.

From time to time, we did see Jack on Apple Street; but the fear that Jack could be run over on the busy street was always present. And then after a month or two not seeing him, we feared the worst. Slowly our memory of Jack became dim. Then it happened! Good news shot up like a dandelion in a crack in the sidewalk. My sister saw Jack slowly limping down our street.

Jack's back! He came by the house and greeted every family member, only to resume his habit of roaming the streets. We accepted the reality that he didn't belong to us, but were happy that he had survived the streets. Then, an incredible ritual began that would last as long as Jack was alive.

As I recall, it began and continued as a nocturnal visit. He never barked that I can recall; he scratched at the front door until someone opened it to let him in. He waited to be greeted, which included petting and a paw shake. At the command, "Give me your paw", he would raise his paw. He would then approach each family member and repeat the ritual. After being greeted by everyone, he would enter every room before he walked to the back of the house. He would then stand by the kitchen door awaiting someone to open it for his departure. I can't recall Jack ever eating when he came to visit. This ritual was repeated for many years until either age or life on the street ended it. After several months of not hearing that familiar scratch at the front door, we knew that we would never hear, "Jack's back" again.

A Remarkable Pet?

Everyone has known a lovable pet who was a one-of-a-kind in some way. The question is in what way was it unique? Was it friendly, faithful, smart or just plain adorable? Cookie, our family mixed breed, was an unremarkable female dog. She was not particularly smart, friendly or endearing. In fact, she was decidedly a pain in the neck. She was a nuisance with which one becomes so familiar that it is hard to imagine your day without her.

Cookie was the name on the adoption papers, but number three son could not pronounce it correctly. He called her "Cho-Cho", the same label he used for the cereal, Cheerios. The name stuck. Thereafter, both the dog and the cereal were called "Cho-Cho", except the cereal was pluralized. I would have chosen a more appropriate name, but my suggestions were always ignored. Cho-Cho had a character flaw buried somewhere in her DNA. I think the name "Bandit" would have been more appropriate. Better yet, "Bandita" would have captured her moral failings and gender.

Cho-Cho had a singular inclination to steal. She would steal my tools, but only when I was using them. Yet her life of crime was coupled with traits of royalty. In short, she behaved like a princess. She was addicted to comfort. She insisted on sleeping next to the clothes dryer, which was almost always on in an inadequate attempt to keep up with the laundry. She was intolerant of drizzle, too much sun, too much cloudiness. At the first sign of any change in the weather, she would shiver in an exaggerated show of discomfort and fear. Her delusion of royalty was aggravating, but most noisome was her blatant acts of theft.

Imagine cutting grass in the sub-tropical heat and humidity as your lawn mower bogs down in the thick thatch. Fertilized by farms of the

Mississippi Valley, river sand is used as fill for the backyards in the New Orleans area. The grass is so thick that birds become trapped in the thick thatch as they forage for food. Further imagine that your mower dies and won't start. You get your tools and begin to investigate, only to reach for your screw driver that has disappeared. Across the yard, you see a hairy thief chewing on it. You slyly maneuver in to steal it back, but she gets wind of your intentions and runs off with it. When you finally retrieve it, she has chewed the hard plastic handle so deeply so that it is uncomfortable to hold. You wonder why you did not notice the theft, so you put it down and play like you are working on the mower. Your incurable thief maneuvers around the yard and approaches from your blind side. With lightning speed, she grabs the tool and runs off. Her petty thievery was a noisome problem, but it was the grand theft that was both impressive and dastardly. That singular act made me question her fidelity.

Rarely were we able to afford porter house steaks, but on that day of infamy, she jumped and stole one from the grill in one clean maneuver and ran off with it. I retrieved it and examined her. I found nothing, not even singed fur. I never forgave her and probably never will.

Robin Hunters

My parents experienced the Great Depression and knew hard times. Even before the bad economy, it was customary to eat the food that flew to you. They would use mouse traps baited with bread to capture birds that fell for the trick. It sounds cruel today, but it was a widespread practice among those who could afford chicken only once a week. But, like most people, they threw table scraps to the birds. However, they had no problem having them over for lunch.

I had permission to hunt birds, but was strictly forbidden to kill them wantonly. My next-door neighbor and I would shoot robins perched in his mother's pecan tree and clean them in his unused garage. My mother would freeze them until there were enough to make a red gravy stew. It would take about 40 bird breasts served over pasta or rice to serve the whole family.

Although we would eat any species large enough, robins were the best. Robins arrived in the New Orleans area every late fall and stayed until the end of winter. Roosting robins would literally cover every branch of the live oaks a few blocks from our yard. We would shoot one and only a score would momentarily leave, only to return to the roost. We could not always roam the streets at night fall. Most of the time we had to rely on our shooting skills during the day. Sometimes, our targets were perched high. With the first shot, the birds would usually fly away or to a higher branch, unless the bb found its target.

When we hunted off our property, we had to swiftly take our kill to the garage to be cleaned. But in our own backyard, we would shoot robins and throw them in the garage and clean them later. We feared some of our neighbors because they threatened to call the police.

A passing police car would send us into panic. We hid the guns and focused on cleaning the garage and hiding the evidence. One day, while cleaning a half dozen robins we saw a police car passing by. Fearing the long arm of the law, we hurried to the garage to erase all evidence of our crimes.

If you ever cleaned birds, you know that there is no way to pick up all the feathers, particularly the down. We tried, but in a very large empty closed space, feathers will scatter. With just a crack in the door for light, the delicate down seemed to hang mid-air.

After working at it for what seemed to be a long time, my friend and partner in crime asked if I thought we had concealed the evidence. Scanning the length and breadth of the garage, it was not hard to discern a bit of enthralls here and there and the downy feathers that seemed to multiply. I declared, "They will never suspect us".

We were not busted. The police showed up and spoke to our parents. We didn't know why they didn't search the garage. We had no idea of constitutional rights. It was only much later in life did we realize that a warrant was required to search private property. I can only imagine what a judge would say had the police requested one.

No Hunting in Traffic Circles

D id you ever regret something and two hours later forgot how much you regretted it? Once the bandmaster's son and I were just hanging around with nothing to do. We decided, as geniuses often do, to go hunting. With only one single shot gun between us, we hitched hiked over the Huey P. Long Bridge. Once we thanked our ride, we looked west and scanned the woods. We were standing in the grassy area in the traffic circle; and the train bridge was directly overhead. At that moment, a train was making its slow but noisy descent. Cars headed in different directions and horns sounded signaling motorists' annoyance. What captured our attention was the sudden stirring of pigeons as the train rattled and shook the trestle.

We noticed that the pigeons were only briefly agitated, for they soon returned to their roost as the train passed. We loaded our gun and we both in turn took shots, hoping that the pellets that struck the trestle would not fall on the passing cars.

It took only a minute or two before police officers noticed our weird hunting habits. I can't remember the conversation we had with the police; I only recall how scarred we both were.

We soon found ourselves huddled together in the back seat of a police car, headed only God knows where. When questioned by the officers, it was all "Yes, Sir" and "No, Sir". When asked with what reception we would be received at home, I believe our body language silently screamed, "We are dead"!

We had ample time to contemplate our fate as the police car crossed over the bridge and emerged on Jefferson Ave. Silently, we crossed the Parish line and Jefferson Ave. becomes Claiborne Ave. As we approached the S. Carrolton Ave. intersection, we sank deeper into despair. Once on Apple St., we knew our unhappy fate was sealed. And then came a miracle!

A block from my father's Shoe Repair Shop, we got a trumpet call of hope. One officer returned our shot gun, sternly reprimanded us and enumerated the things that would befall us were we to repeat our offence. Now, you would think that after dodging a bullet, you would hang low for a while.

But once we realized that we would not be counted among the dead, our thoughts quickly turned to filling in what remained of the day with fun things to do. After reviewing our options and keenly aware of our recent experience, we decided to go hunting. We did learn our lesson. This time we would be discreet. We visualized being discreet, because the word was not in our vocabulary. When we hitched hiked back to the scene of the crime, we avoided the traffic circle and hunted the woods nearby.

I have always wondered why the police let us off with a warning. Do you suppose that our stupidity reminded them of their youthful folly? I read somewhere that seeing ourselves in a different guise is the trigger to compassion.

Secrets You Keep from Kids

E verybody has done something really stupid in childhood. The preferred phraseology today is "bad choice". Professionals recommend that you allow your children to see your limitations. They believe that it is good to admit to them that you also have made bad choices. But I believe that your children's security requires that you keep silent. Let's cut to the chase. I did some really stupid things in childhood and I'll bet most readers did too. However, I would advise the reader not to tell their children the really stupid things they did until their children are at least forty.

I don't recall who among my friends suggested the brilliant idea that we roller skate down the Huey P. Long Bridge, but I don't think I did. Now the Bridge was built during the Great Depression to accommodate the narrow vehicles of that time. It is high and steep and motorists will go out of their way to avoid using it. The overhead train tracks are used by slow but noisy freight trains. The sound of clatter and vibration from trains is another reason some motorist wish to avoid the thrill of the Bridge.

The skates used in the 1950s were made of steel with a leather strap. They attached to your shoe and had ball bearing wheels. Union skates could be adjusted for length and width, provided you had the adjustment tool that was shaped like a key. I thank God we didn't have modern shoe skates, which are extremely fast and expensive. But better skates were unknown to us, so we took what we had in search of a thrill.

We walked up the Bridge with skates in hand. As we approached the highest point as it begins its descent, we fastened our skates and stayed close to the curb in single file. For a split second, we were on fire, or at least our skates were. And then, the wheels turned so fast that the friction turned them into sparks of fire. The casing that held the bearings disintegrated and the steel balls in the bearings spilled out and rolled down the Bridge. The thrill lasted no more than a few seconds, but not before an angry trucker yelled unfriendly words at us.

To think of all the planning that went into this adventure, it hardly seems worth it. We lost our skates and were roundly insulted by truckers in exchange for a few seconds of fun. Unfortunately, without skates, we could not recapture the moment. When "the stupids" came over us again, it was an adventure that could be repeated.

I promised my wife that I would not tell our children that I rode a falling tree and survived to repeat it. The origin of these adventures is a mystery. Who tries it first, survives and suggests it to others? I have a theory that no one does, it's a collective effort. The idea of an adventure springs from a collective imagination, but requires salesmanship to convince others that it will be fun and can be survived.

To perform the daring act of stupidity and ride a falling tree, you need two things. A hand axe and a forest are prerequisites for this adventure. The axe must be sharp and the forest a medium density of small and mid-size trees. You scout the area and select the tree that will be slowed in its descent by nearby trees. Under usual conditions, a tree is felled only if a clean fall to the ground is possible. But riding trees requires a different strategy.

When you think you have chosen wisely, you ask your friends for confirmation. There can be and usually are diverse opinions. Questions arise over the size of the tree, whether its branches will slow its fall. Endless discussions follow, but eventually a tree is chosen and the chopping begins. At some point in the chopping process, you must decide if the cut is deep enough for the tree to break with repeated jumps after ascent, but not so deep that the tree falls before you ascend. When the tree comes to a stop and is inclined at a 45 to 60-degree angle, you carefully climb it and shake the tree until it begins to fall.

When done poorly, the ride is slow enough to be almost safe. When done correctly, it is fast enough to be dangerous and fun. And this is why I insist that there is a difference between making a bad choice and being stupid. Readers! I implore you! Do not allow your children under 59 years old to read this snippet!

On to Mexico

It doesn't take much brains for three biology students to organize a field trip to Mexico. All you need is a little cash, reliable old Chevy and determination to return with cool specimens. In fact, brains would have slowed us down or prematurely terminated the trip. Before leaving New Orleans, fully operational brain cells would have directed us to check the weather forecast, after all hurricanes are common in late summer and fall. But we didn't and we encountered and unexpected one near New Iberia, Louisiana. Fortunately, we drove pass the bad weather, dodging wind -born debris unscathed, except for lost wiper blades. But, we didn't really need them in sun soaked Mexico.

By the time we had reached McAllen, Texas, we were tired and so was the Chevy. We decided that the bird sanctuary south of Mc Allen would be a great place to bed over. A couple hundred yards from the Rio Grande was a nice spot to set up camp and plan for the trip ahead. But our retreat into nature was repeatedly disturbed by the unsolicited visits from homo sapiens. First the custodian of the bird sanctuary and then by his wife came to warn of the dangers of our "nice spot". Several times were we warned about the "wetbacks", Mexicans who chose to swim across the River to the US side of the River rather than follow the road signs. No one would have imagined then that in the future there would be more swimmers than road travelers.

Too weary or scared to argue, we parked the chevy in a covered parking slot adjacent to the custodian's residence. In a flash, we fell asleep and night turned into morning. And in a New York second, we were given two surprises, one very pleasant and one not so much.

Breakfast at curb side was served in generous Texan style. What a welcomed surprise! But, not so wonderful was the explosion of countless birds of every description, size and language. Unknown to us, they assembled the night before filling every tree branch in the sanctuary. It was not the sounds of gentle song birds in happy bird speak. No! This was the screaming of a multitude of birds in full throated argument. After expressing our gratitude for the wonderful breakfast, we left Texas for the quiet of Mexico.

Still on to Mexico

As we crossed the River into Mexico, we were very glad not to hear the bird arguments that we had heard North of the River. My first emotion, once we cleared the congestion at the border was a bit of surprise. Funny, Mexico looks just like Texas, but that was about to change as the flood plain gave way to lofty heights.

So, this is Mexico and not the border sprawl that we had left behind. All morning the Chevy snaked its' way around the twists and turns; no sight of people or cars. Nervously, we negotiated the eight-kilometer speed limit turns and precipitous drop offs. After many white-knuckle turns, the horizon opened and the town below beckoned us to stop.

We were thirsty and China looked like a good place to get a drink. Mexican cokes right out of a coke machine did the job of slaking our thirst and a moment to take in China with its' multicolored buildings. No two adjacent walls were the same color. All the bold colors of earth. sky and town seemed to make one uniform picture.

China was not the town referenced in the "hecho in China" written on products destined for Spanish speakers.

The whole point of the trip was to collect cool specimens. That we did, including butterflies, tortoises, tarantulas and other creatures including plants. In our hunt for anything, we were chased out of a corn field by a motorcycle patrolman. With only a few butterflies captured, we moved on to our final stop, Monterey.

By the time we reached the outskirts of Monterey, ensuing darkness was our signal to pull over and sleep. As evening wore on the sun set the landscape ablaze. But, at length the only light we could see was the city lights and the only sounds were the argumentative parakeets in the trees next to the Chevy. Sleep came without warning and so did wakefulness.

The quiet night passed and gave way to the noise and sights of first light. Seemingly from nowhere emerged buses and riders converging on the highway. Were all these people hiding behind cacti? I saw no one the previous day. Mysteries, notwithstanding, we followed the cars and overcrowded buses to Monterey.

Monterey is no sleepy metropolis, but a busy convergence of multicolored vehicles. Older models of American cars are given new life and color. We could stay in Monterey only a few hours, for our food and cash were nearly gone. A cold treat and then back on the road to the USA in the old Chevy stuffed with specimens. Then came the border surprise.

Everyone in the world conspired against us and hid the law that prohibits certain animals and plants to cross the border into United States. So, we took this disappointment in stride and preceded to catch the same specimens in Texas.

Catching Snakes for Fun

Most people, if not afraid, are at least a little leery of snakes. But to some, snakes are both beautiful and interesting, but not too many. I read somewhere that the sudden appearance of a snake causes panic in a troupe of monkeys. My initial feeling toward snakes mirrors that of primates. So why catch snakes? Could it have something to do with the push from boyhood to manhood? It's best to leave such questions to experts. I can only relate my own experience.

I don't remember how it started, but one day an older boy showed my friends and I a snake. He told us how and where he caught it. My friends were fascinated. I was both intrigued and anxious. In a transparent display of "machoness", we were told that real snake catchers don't use snake sticks on non-poisonous snakes. It appears, that "machoness" has its limits.

The technique explained to us was both simple and graceful when performed in one seamless movement. Confronted snakes normally flee, unless they are cornered. As the snake slithers away, you grab it by the tail, raise it two or three feet off the ground and quickly hurl it between your parted legs. You clamp your legs together and the snake becomes disoriented. At this point, you simply pull the snake toward the front of you until you can reach its head. In a flash, you have the snake in your hand. The fact that it is easier to simply pick up the snake and put in a pillow case is beside the point. The whole point is to create a "wow" response. Later in life, I would use this technique to impress my high school biology class, my children and my grandchildren. It can be both impressive and dangerous, not to the catcher, but to the snake.

Incidents I recall when I made my debut in snake catching reveal the potential danger. Several times, I hesitated when I raised the snake in mid-air. It turned its head toward me with its mouth agape. In that split second, I imagined that it was a poisonous snake and dropped it. Convinced that my impression was wrong, I picked it up and tried again, only to be overcome by the same fear. It is my recollection that I caught and cast down the same snake three times before it escaped for good.

All my fear was focused on my safety with no concern for the snake. I did not realize that the quick change of directions required to secure the snake could be deadly. Once, I grabbed the snake and jerked it back toward my parted legs with such force that I cracked its spine. The poor creature was permanently deformed into a right angle. I felt bad and really ashamed.

Catching Snakes for Profit

There is nothing better than having a jingle in your pocket that you earned yourself, even more so when you can do it in collaboration with friends. My friend and I each would commandeer a pillow case from home and go to "work". With pillow cases in hand, we began by walking to Claiborne Avenue with our thumbs pointed West. Once you cross the Parish line, Claiborne becomes Jefferson Avenue (US 90) and traverses the Mississippi by way of the Huey P. Long Bridge. Once on the Westbank, we entered the nearby woods and began "work".

Only feet from the highway, we would typically catch ribbon snakes for which we were paid ten cents a-piece. But the real money was in the very abundant water snakes in the nearby swampy areas. We got fifty cents a pound for the larger snakes. It wouldn't take long before our pillow cases were wreathing and bulging with assorted water snakes. Then our thoughts turned to the money we expected from Maclung's Snake Farm. But first, we had to get our snakes home. It was always easy to hitch a ride without snakes, but with snakes, it could take a little time. Not only is it difficult to explain why the pillow case you are carrying moves, but snakes stink because they dispel a really obnoxious anal gland secretion to discourage predators.

We tried to keep the snakes still so as to not call attention to them. There wasn't much we could do about the smell. It could take a good walk along the highway before a vehicle would stop to pick up kids with snakes. Once, a nice lady stopped, but enquired about our pillow cases. When she realized there were snakes in our sacks, she informed us that the snakes had to ride in the trunk.

I don't know when we decided that it was inefficient to catch snakes on Highway 90 because the snake farm was located in Laplace on Highway 61. It made more sense to catch snakes near the vendor, since snakes are abundant in Southeast Louisiana anywhere there are canals, ditches, ponds and swamps.

Maclung's Snake Farm was a tourist attraction for the visitors to New Orleans, which is only short car ride away. Tourist could see a variety of snakes and alligators and watch young ladies handle deadly cobras. Several years later I was volunteering at Charity Hospital and in the emergency room when a state trooper brought a cobra bitten handler from the Snake Farm. Unfortunately, the young lady didn't survive.

There was more to see than exotic animals and pretty ladies handling cobras. Slot machines, or as they were called then, one-armed bandits, were tucked away in closets and small rooms. Gambling was illegal at the time, and Louisiana was experiencing a "reform" which was ultimately doomed to fail. But with our earnings from snake sales, we enthusiastically sought out the hidden slots. For as long as I can remember, gambling of all types was deeply entrenched in South Louisiana. Even kids were allowed to play pinball machines that payed off. I can remember doing so on my lunch hour in grade school, usually with the same outcome as playing the slots with earnings from snake sales.

Bull Attack

Angry bulls are very intimidating, particularly Brahman bulls with that scary hump on their back. I got attacked by one while minding my own business fishing in the spillway. I was a teenager at the time and my newfound favorite place was the spillway just northwest of New Orleans. What a stretch of land! You could hunt, fish, catch crawfish and crabs and pasture your cattle. Its history is tied to the cycle of floods affecting the New Orleans area.

Just upriver from New Orleans near the town of Norco, an eighteenth-century crevasse caused serious flooding. The Mississippi poured over the area, flooding farms and homes. The US Army Corp of Engineers eventually put a stop to the breeches in the levee by building a control structure at the site of the old breech. On both flanks, levees were raised from the Mississippi River to Lake Pontchartrain. The flood gates have been opened many times to lower the water levee in the River. What a bonanza! Rich top soil from the entire Mississippi Valley is deposited with every opening. Builders get river sand, wildlife is nourished, and cattle have rich pasture. And all of this is lagniappe for protecting the City from floods. And the mention of cattle brings me back to the bull attack.

In my concentration on fishing, I hadn't heard the rustle of cattle until a bull began to grunt and curse me out. I turned around and saw one of the largest beasts I had ever seen. I tried to be nonchalant and not look afraid. But my body didn't lie as well as my lips. Valor called for immediate action. I picked up my tackle box and went into the drink. The bull, for his part, stopped at the water's edge. I was safe, but I forgot to latch my box, and tackle scattered in a trail to the water. To this day, every time I pick up an unlatched tackle box, I remember the bull but still can't seem to remember to latch my tackle box.

More Bull

For reasons unknown to me, bulls and cows appear when you least expect and want them to. Sometimes as lovable large nuisances and other times as potential danger. I really didn't mind it when a neighbor's cow decided to sample the grass in my front yard. But when they interfere with my fishing, I get upset. And when they threaten to crush me, my fishing buddy and his car, I get very mad and fearful.

Me and my fellow graduate student at LSU decided to go fishing. So, we packed his little Volkswagen bug and off we went seeking fame and fortune, but willing to settle for fish and crawfish. When we got to Ramah, Louisiana, we parked on top the levee that keeps the water of the Atchafalaya Basin at bay. We caught fish immediately and knew it was going to be a good day. As I was reeling in a fish, I noticed a few cattle eating grass on the levee coming to pay us a visit. A few more fish later, my fishing buddy remarks, "Looks like the whole herd is on the levee!" Our amusement quickly turned into anxiety. "Are they bumping into my car?" We picked up our fish and ran to the car, there were three or four bovine friends near it. By the time we packed our gear and started the engine, we were surrounded. Neither the noise of the horn nor the roar of the engine dispersed them. Pretty soon, we were surrounded on all sides. As more cattle entered the scene, the car rocked as the herd swelled on all sides. We could not drive away or open the doors. We were forced to wait, hoping that the crush of cattle would not knock us down the levee and into the water.

Eventually, the herd relented, and we were able to slowly drive down the levee. But, we had to follow a path of least resistance, weaving in openings that appeared and quickly disappeared. Once on the road, our noses directed us to a crawfish market, a stone's throw away. Live crawfish at five cents a pound was a real bargain. Life is good! Homeward bound, we left in haste to enjoy the good life with our friends. And that's no bull.

Making Groceries

I like grocery shopping for groceries or as we say in New Orleans, "making groceries". I suppose I am one of a handful of people who really do. I find interacting with people as they shop for groceries amusing. I delight in the sight and smells of produce neatly packed on display shelves. But like most people I don't enjoy the big surprise at check out. Generally, I suppose that about now you are probably saying to yourself, "This guy needs a life". Some people believe that you have to be miserable most of the time to have a life, but I don't. However, if you prefer to hear about bad experiences, I have one to offer.

As a family of ten, we had to shop with two carts, one for my wife and one for me. After more than an hour of shopping, I turned around to place one last item in my cart and low and behold my cart was gone and so was hers. We searched the store from front to back, side to side, but they had vanished. We even asked the store manager to assist us. But the carts and all our groceries were gone! To this day, the missing shopping carts remain an unsolved mystery. The store manager's theory was that a confused shopper, absentmindedly took them. If so, how do explain a tin of pipe tobacco to your husband, assuming that the distracted shopper was a woman? If the shopper was a male... The mind reels with the many possibilities. I decided long ago that it is best to leave life's mysteries unsolved. But some apparent mysteries aren't mysteries, they are solvable puzzles, like the inconsolable toddler in a supermarket.

Toddlers can be big trouble grocery shopping. If they get fussy, the temptation to give them junk food can be overpowering. First, they demand everything they see, then they cry until you let them eat it. It's a lot easier if you and your spouse shop together. If not, you can expect a cross examination when you return home. "Honey, why are so many cookie bags and boxes opened"?

It is difficult to watch a distraught mother intimidated by a two-year old tyrant. You want to help, but you feel helpless. Do you just walk up to her and say, "Ma'am, may I distract your kid while you finish shopping"? Faced with that dilemma, I came up with a creative solution. I practiced therapy without a license on crying toddlers in supermarkets, until my more prudent wife put an end to it.

The technique I used was both simple and effective. I hear the tell-tale sounds of a temper tantrum and move my cart in position. I see the open bags of goodies and the look of desperation on mother's face. I hide behind an end cap and jiggle the keys on my key ring. Once I am convinced that the child hears the noise and momentarily stops crying, I stop. When I am sure I can distract the toddler on cue, I maneuver my cart so as to be in full view of his mother. I repeat the procedure several times until I am convinced that the child's mother sees that uncontrollable crying can be stooped by the noise of keys. Without knowing whether or not she understands, I depart, hoping for her sake that she has the determination to face her diminutive tyrant. Unfortunately, I know longer help distressed mothers. My wife convinced me that I am either going to get myself arrested or committed.

Phycology, Say What?

P hycology is the study of algae and to a botanist, are interesting primitive plants. Giant kelps are found in the seas, but microscopic varieties inhabit both fresh and salt waters. And some have glass cell walls in shapes that mock human imagination. Not only are they commercially important, but are a valuable food source. Next time you eat sushi, try not to think of it as seed weed or pond scum.

I took a graduate class in phycology and besides lab study, field trips were required. I was the sole student that semester and the head of the department and I went across

the River to the Westwego area. In a short period of trekking, we collected several samples of algae worthy for the return trip to the lab. I don't remember any particularly exciting specimens, but I knew from previous experience that if you search Louisiana swamps carefully, you can expect to find almost anything. On more than one occasion, I found creatures that simply were not in any field manual. Neither I nor my professor had a clue to their identity. With the expectation of finding something exciting, we continued our search. We were just about to give up and be satisfied with what we had. when rustling noises drew our attention from the water to the nearby woods.

Suddenly, two suited men donning white shirts and ties, appeared. At first, we were startled, then we were apprehensive. There were no roads around and we had to walk a good distance through a swampy area to reach the place. I thought to myself, "Well, if I am going to meet my Maker, it is good that I have a priest here to hear my last confession". My professor was a Jesuit Priest and Chair of the Biology Department. Of course, he was in field collecting clothes and these men couldn't have known that he was a priest and it probably wouldn't have mattered.

Only one of the two gentlemen spoke. "This is Carlos Marcello's private property", he said with the suggestion in his voice that we should leave. And leave we did. My professor was strangely silent on our way back to the University. Later I would learn that the property did indeed belong to Carlos Marcello, the reputed head of the Dixie Mafia. Much later in life as a sociologist, I interviewed the FBI agent who wire tapped Marcello's phone. The evidence that Marcello was planning to kill Robert Kennedy was less than flimsy. Speaking of the grief that the Attorney General was giving him, he used a Sicilian expression. "When you want to kill a rooster, you don't pluck off his tail, you chop off his head." Had the government proved that he headed a crime family, I could have rightly boasted. "I faced the Mafia for the sake of science"!

What to cook. what to cook. what to cook?

Wild Pigs

Where would we be without pigs? The exclusion of pigs for dietary or religious reasons is quite common and understandable. Did you ever watch pigs wallow in slop? Those who fancy bacon are unfazed by this apparent lack of hygiene. The same can be said of people who are devotees of mud bugs (crawfish). But pigs can be downright ornery, particularly wild ones. My encounters with pigs stretchers over a lifetime.

My first encounter was when I was a graduate student working on the ecology of temporary ponds. My major Professor, Water Moore, was a world authority on fairy shrimp, tiny shrimp that only inhabit temporary bodies of water. So extraordinary are they that enterprising entrepreneurs sell them as "water monkeys". Their eggs can last for decades out of water, surviving in the dry soil. Hatching begins with robust rains, and the cycle of life continues. But not until a playground for feral pigs is created.

My job was to take samples of the fauna in the water, as well as temperature and oxygen levels. But before I could do that, I had to get to the water. Often, this was no easy task when a herd of swine was guarding their playground. They would grunt and form their offensive and defensive phalanx. Most often, I chose the courteous action and simply waited for my turn to get into the water. The student that preceded me in this role used his forty-five and scared them out the water. There were times that I encountered only one or two in the nearby woods on my way to the pond. These encounters left an indelible memory.

When you are an uninvited guest to a sow and her piglets' foraging party, both the disturbed and the disturber are frightened. She squealed, and I jumped and ran to the nearest tree. She was large and angry and charged, but I was half way up the tree before she came close. I don't know how long I clung to that pine tree, but it seemed like forever. What I do know is that, when it was safe to come down, I couldn't tell which direction led to the road and my car.

It was embarrassing; I couldn't find my way out. Some of my children say that I am still lost somewhere in the woods of Southeast Louisiana. I learned that fear can rob you of your wits, provided that you have some.

Penny Party

Neighborhood penny parties were a cross between a block party and a small-scale festival. There were make shift stages set up for skits, actors in costumes, food and drinks, games of chance along with the popular games of the day.

Mothers' who were enlisted, pulled out their family recipes of goodies. My sister-in-law's mother made fudge and there were cookies and candy. Everyone drank the drink du jour, very sweet Kool aid.

The games were those popular in 1940s and 1950s, like yo-yos and tops. And who can forget the games played with baseball cards? They were thrown toward a wall and the player who got closest, won all the cards thrown. A whiskey jigger placed in a five-gallon pickle jar filled with water offered a challenge to drop a penny and have it fall in the jigger to win a prize. Grab bags with small toys wrapped in brown paper offered certain success.

Some of the prizes were small toys saved from Cracker Jack boxes. Almost untouched second-hand trinkets found here and about wound up as prizes. Small toys offered by cereal makers, for the price of box tops, also accounted for some of the prizes. I was always amazed by the sudden appearance of prizes and the eagerness of kids contributing to the success of a penny party. I have no recollection of how penny parties were organized. It was a collaborative effort drawn from the talent at hand. Yet, special talented kids stepped forward to ply their theatrical artistry.

I recall my mother's absolute thrill to get her fortune told by a neighborhood teenage "fortune teller". For a mere penny, she was told facts about her life that everyone in the neighborhood knew by heart.

"Mrs. Margavio you are a married woman and you have five children". It was the costuming and theatrical props that made the whole thing a tour de force. My favorite experience, besides grab bags and drop the penny in the whisky jigger was the master skit.

The skit itself had no real story line. It challenged the audience to guess the real identity of the masked and fully costumed super hero. One could not solve the mystery by a simple process of elimination, since the super hero appeared on stage only briefly. After dispensing with mask and costume, he could disappear in the crowd as part of a bewildered audience. However, one year, the organizers committed a fatal flaw.

They selected the only kid in the neighborhood with a lame right arm. In early childhood, the super hero's right arm was caught in a washing machine wringer. As a result of this accident, he was unable to straighten his elbow. When walking, his right arm moved as if in a sling. Had this lapse of judgement not been made, I probably would not have such fond memories of our neighborhood penny parties.

A Neighbor's Reproach

I t was a hot and humid summer day as I emerged from my home carrying tools, followed by three small sons. My plan was to repair the family station wagon with, of course, the assistance of three sons. Since the car was parked on the street, I kept one eye on the task at hand and the other eye on my full-time job of keeping my sons safe. Without warning, my across-the-street neighbor interrupted my concentration, and the reason for this unexpected visit was both surprising and insulting.

He had interrupted his busy schedule and my concentration to address an important matter. Without preamble or excuse, he directly confronted me. "You have too many children!", he said. He immediately walked across the street to his home and, no doubt, his busy work load. My over taxed brain reeled in a landslide of emotions. After resisting the temptation to throw a wrench at him, a light shone through the darkness as I recalled some wisdom a university colleague imparted to me a year earlier.

Using the principle of moderation in stoic philosophy, with more tact than my neighbor, he gave the same advice. Scales fell from my eyes in the convergence of advice from divergent sources. Oddly, my neighbor in the pest control business and a university professor are telling me how to live my life. I nurtured the guidance and reflected on its deepest meaning. On the spot, I vowed to mend my ways and direct my life according to the philosophy of moderation. But, then I realized that it was too late for one approaching the evening of life. It was not too late, however, for moderation to inform life for my children. I will tell my children and instruct them on the dangers of immoderation. So urgent was my message that I began to rehearse my speech to them as if it were my last opportunity to do so.

In my mind's eyes, I stood before them as if I were in the lecture hall before a sea of students. "Children, listen to your father. I wish to impart sound wisdom to you." Fearing that, given their tender years, they would not understand, I simplified my lecture.

"Children, your father wishes you to follow the path set by the stoic philosophy of moderation, which was lived out by the great Roman emperor, Marcus Aurelias. I shall focus on three areas: love, virtue and work. With regard to love, do not love persons or things with abandonment. Rather, strive for detachment and moderate your love. Do this, and your friend that calls for help in the middle of the night will never disturb your sleep. With regard to virtue, generally be chase, but do so with moderation. Be moderate, don't let chastity ruin your Saturday night. With regard to work, do not strive for excellence. There will be time that others will tempt you to excel. Do not listen to this formula for disaster. You would do well to strive for mediocrity, which is the sure guide for happiness. Listen children and abide by the words of your father. In all things, moderation is the best path to follow. Follow my advice and you will live long and happy lives."

Got Problems?

So, what's a problem? I suppose the answer depends on one's point of view. The first time I encountered a claimed "problem" that wasn't a problem, from my point of view, was when I was a young teacher with three small children. A good friend and Dean encountered me in a hallway and began to speak. I could tell by his demeanor that he had a weighty subject on his mind. Or was it on his sleeve?

"Look here", he said. He pointed to his right sleeve. He explained that there was a rogue thread that the stem of his watch snagged. He illustrated this unfortunate state of affairs by showing me just how it happened. To make matters worse, the shirt was a present from his mother-in-law. From his point of view, this was a tragedy for which there was no solution. Unkind thoughts raced through my brain and I forced myself not to give them expression. What I wanted to say was, "You big dummy. Do you have any idea how easy you have it?" In my mind's eyes I was comparing his lot to mine. He knew nothing of the problems encountered when raising a family with small children. Instead of voicing these feelings, I did my best commiserating. Nothing more was said, but I probably did mention this to another friend and my wife. I can't explain why such a trivial incident resides in my memory decades later. Unless, it persists as a parable for my illumination. Is it possible that the same can be said of my problems? Have I been convicted by my own words?

Neither of us had a real problem, even when we thought we had. We didn't face grinding poverty, chronic poor health or other problems so many people face. I summon this memory whenever I need perspective. It has been helpful, and I offer it to the reader. Rather than condemning my friend for his silliness, I thank him for the light that dispatches my self-made darkness.

Phone Problems

What would we do without mobile phones? A mobile phone is a wonderful thing. You can reach out to a friend or get help in an emergency. Of course, you can make out like a bird and tweet your life away or get distracted and crash your car. However, on the whole, a mobile phone is a dandy thing. But in the hands of a teenager, it can be a scary thing. How serious can it be? The reader must decide.

Number five son received a call from an unknown caller, but entered into conversation anyway. The party calling was a plumber seeking guidance from his boss. In most cases, receivers of mistaken calls simply say, "You got the wrong number", and hang up. But if your brain is not fully operational, you start talking just to see where the conversation might go. Usually, it doesn't go very far before one party hangs up. My teenager decided to take it as far as possible, and this is the scary part.

The plumber, thinking that he is speaking to his boss, says, "Do you want to replace the pipe just in the back, or do you want me to go all the way to the street?" As everybody knows, when you replace a pipe, you tear up the old one and everything that is in your way. Demolition is unforgiving, and the mess and expense involved are serious. So, what does number five son do? He answers the plumber's question.

"Yeah, run the pipe all the way to the street", he tells the plumber. "Okay", the plumber replies. I was informed of these goings on days after the event. I had no way of undoing what my son did. In fact, there was no way of knowing if the plumber actually did anything. I know nothing. I don't even know where the rogue demolition was to take place.

For days, pictures of destruction crossed my mind. In my imagination, I was present to witness the conversation between the plumber and his boss. "Why the hell did you tear up the place?" "You told me too!" "I didn't tell you that!" "You told me to when I called you." It was a big relief when I realized that, had the destruction actually taken place, I could not be held legally responsible.

Three Little Piggies and a Bomb

Many mysteries can be solved through scientific examination. Others, like a child's mind, are best celebrated. Now most adults are simply too busy with important matters to enjoy the thoughts and words of children. On the whole, grandparents have more time and interest in what their grandchildren say and do. Perhaps, wisdom does come with age or possibly we just get silly as we age. But grandparents usually have more time to appreciate unimportant things. An example might help to clarify my meaning.

Sometime ago, as my wife and I were getting in our car in the parking lot of a home improvement store, an unusual scene caught my attention. In the middle of the lot was a young woman and small child balancing on parking barriers. I assumed they were mother and daughter playing a very popular sport among the three-year old set. The mother struck me as only a half-hearted player. I don't believe she was giving it her full attention. For all I know her mind might have been fixed on some important purchase which drew her to the store in the first place.

I started my engine to exit the lot and remarked to my wife that it is fun to balance on parking lot barriers. I then posed a deep philosophical question. What is more important, a purposeful action or a useless fancy? I voted for fancy. My wife agreed, but I believe she just didn't want to hear any more of my foolishness.

The brief episode and one-sided conversation made me reflect on an incident of child's play that I will not soon forget. I was playing with my granddaughter Emily and acting out nursery rhymes. Following her directions, I was a piggy who built a straw house and she was the big bad wolf who was to blow it down and run after me. Of course,

I joined my brother in his house of sticks. And as the story goes, we are visited by the wolf, who huffs and puffs and blows our house in. Unfortunately, this is where my granddaughter's version departs from the original. In her version, the wolf is also able to blow down the brick house. Each time I had my home blown down, I had to run away from the pursuing wolf.

Being a part-time genius, it became obvious to me that for her the fun was in the chase. A long time passed and my legs grew weary. It was only then that I began to gripe and complain. In the hopes of getting a little rest, I told her that the wolf could not blow down a brick house. She adamantly insisted that the wolf could. I told her that it was not possible for a wolf to blow down a brick house and there was nothing more to be said on the subject. With complete disregard for fidelity to the original story, she added her own twist. "Well, the wolf has got one of those things. You know; they make a loud noise and go boom". As she waved her hands about to illustrate a bomb exploding, she searched her memory for the right word. I said, "You mean a bomb"? "Yea, a bomb".

Fishing Stories

The words fishing and story go together like beans and rice. Fishing is a story. When you plan to go fishing you never know what story will emerge. Of course, many people assume that a fishing story is almost always a tall tale about a large fish that got away. Is a fishy story fishy because it is a fish tale? I defer to the reader to decide whether the following tales are fishy.

Once I was fly fishing with two sons in a small boat. Trying to reach the bank, I hung the fly in a tree. Unfortunately, the fly was entangled on a branch that was home to a yellow jacket hive, that can best be described as the mother of all nests. I didn't see the nest and continued to pull and jerk my rod in the hopes that I could retrieve my fly. In seconds, we were engulfed by bees that stung repeatedly. Number four son was at the helm and was spared. Unlucky son number five sustained multiple stings as did I. He kept saying, "Just go...just go"! We screamed at number four son to get out of Dodge. Unfortunately, he was laughing so hard, he was in no condition to make a speedy retreat. I vowed to get even, but never did. From that time on, I always inspected trees nearby and stood ready to cut my line. We survived to fish again, but a fishing trip is always a new story in progress waiting to be told.

I recall an unbelievable trip we took to Bayou Segnette. Ever since the eco-tours were launched, I was a bit leery of fishing there. The tourists were found of feeding alligators. Every time the gators heard boat motors; they would come for supper. Ordinarily, gators simply shy away, but when they are conditioned to eat at the sound of a boat motor, you never know what they might do if you fell into the water.

These thoughts crossed my mind while fishing in a spot frequented by eco-tours, I was leaning on a large tree trunk sticking six feet out the water. I was wearing my new fishing hat my mother-in-law had bought me. My pipe was in my mouth and my eye glasses firmly in place. I leaned on the rotten tree trunk too long; it snapped and I fell into the drink. The only thing I could think of was those eco-tours and gators. I yelled for my son to help, but he was laughing so hard that it took him some time before he could rescue me. When I was finally able to climb back into the boat. I took inventory. My glasses were still there, my pipe was still held tightly in place, but my new hat was gone. I had lost a new hat and my dignity. But I did have a fish story to tell and I didn't have to exaggerate the size or number of fish caught.

Bedtimes and Other Stories

It's not easy putting five little boys to bed. Of course, you tell several bed times stories. When that doesn't work, you use lethal force, verbal threats or tell more stories. The older ones are easy to correct, but what works on a nine-year old may not work on a three-year old. Number six son was difficult to correct. One night, after telling several stories, he still would not observe bedtime silence. I was really upset. I said, "I'm going to give you a spanking". Defiantly, he stood up, raised his little hand and threatened me. "I'm gonna...I'm gonna". I stood my ground and bravely asked, "What are you gonna do"? He looked at me, his hand still raised and said, "I'm gonna... I'm gonna'. Then a long pause ensued, his head drooped and both arms were raised. He continued speaking. "I'm gonna... I'm gonna luv ya". He then embraced me. I eventually got even. He now has children who are genetically programmed to say, "No". Sometimes it's not disobedience, it's just weirdness that gets you.

When I remodeled the kitchen, I removed the upper part of the wall. When you entered the kitchen from the outside side door, you could see any person taller than four feet in the den. One day, returning from work I entered the kitchen and to my right, I spied a baby doll going up and down where the wall once was. I saw nothing else, but I heard a little voice repeatedly saying, "Baba flies...baba flies". I walked into the den and found my two-year old, number seven son, sitting on the sofa. Later in life, he would design and build sensors used in satellites flying into deep space. But, before you are an engineer, you must pass first grade.

His grades were excellent, but something frightened him. We heard no complaints from his teacher. I knew from experience that you must attend to fear as soon as possible. I entered into deep conversation with him to get to the root of the problem. His teacher was a rather tall woman whose previous teaching experience was in an inner-city school. She yelled a lot at disobedient children. "Are you afraid that she might hurt you"? I asked. His answer was an unambiguous, no. "Then why are you afraid"? "I am afraid that she might hurt one of the children". I put my therapy cap on and tried to sever the connection between yelling and hitting. I told him the following: "You see son, all the people who want to teach are put into a room. Then, the principle asks them to scream as loud as they can. The person who screams the loudest gets the job". This may have helped him and the fact that the principle directed her teacher to ease up, didn't hurt.

The Way Kids Think

H ave you ever noticed that little kids don't think like older kids or grown-ups? Speech is not always used to communicate with others. It is often used simply to summon a response in themselves. When my number one son was about three years-old, he asked me a very unsettling question. "Daddy what is the truth"? I paused and pondered whether I should risk an answer. As the words fell from my lips, I was so frustrated with my answer that I simply gave up. In desperation, I said, "It's like when you're not lying". I was surprised that my answer resonated. His body was animated and his eyes revealed that my words found their mark. With great excitement, he said, "Oh lions, they bite you".

When number one was five or six, he was with me as I selected meat for supper. He was an early reader, but I suspected that he would have difficulty with spelling. I picked up a loin steak and put it down, after seeing the price. As we both looked over the steaks, he suddenly became excited. He pointed to a package and said, "Daddy! Daddy, look, lion meat"!

One day, the same son approached me and said, "Snakes bite you"! To which, I replied, "Yes they do". Believing that he wanted to engage me in conversation about snakes, I continued to speak. When I saw him runoff, distracted by other things, I realized that he really didn't want to speak to me about snakes. What he wanted to do was call up the emotions he attaches to snakes. In this regard, young minds are very different. Their thoughts often take unexpected turns.

Once I stopped at a gas station to look for junk food. His sharp eyes spied a shiny silver dollar on the floor. It was the first silver dollar he had ever seen. With unbridled excitement, his eyes fixed on that coin and said, "I would like to see the bubble gum that you get with this nickel"!

My experience with young minds leads me to warn the reader to avoid clichés when speaking to children. Young ones will take a cliché literally. If you say, "Keep your eye on the ball", at batting practice, don't be surprised if the kid picks up the ball and holds it next to his eye. What follows will be the kid's complete bewilderment of how that advice can be followed. Furthermore, literal interpretations can turn your clichés into legal traps.

Once, I was a bit late in giving number four son his allowance. He repeatedly asked for it. His mother was annoyed and she told him, "Don't speak about allowance again"! Shortly thereafter, he returned with a large piece of paper on which was written: "Where is my alloenz"?

Girls Are Different

The facts are in, girls and boys are different. An explosion of literature in genetics and neuroscience has pointed to many differences and similarities. As a former college teacher and the father of seven boys and one girl, I have always had an interest in the subject. My professional background did not include that focus; however, I have done some work in demography and have always been interested in birth and death rates. It is difficult to fully explain why males die at higher rates. Once, I asked my class if anyone wished to explain. One student suggested that males have more fatal accidents because they are stupid. Despite her illumination. I still can't get my head around it and probably never will. Why are males more inclined to experience fatal accidents, even at the age of one and under? What I do know is that my only daughter was different from her brothers.

When it came to danger, I can't recall a single incident when one of my sons warned anybody, including me. I don't have a single recollection of any of them sounding a cautionary note. However, they were all quite eager to report just how stupid and dangerous certain behaviors are, after an accident.

Did any of them warm me or hold the ladder when it fell while I was trying to get down from the roof? And did they warn me when I fell off the ladder while holding an electric drill building their tree house? And when I burnt down a bush by emptying my pipe on it; did they hold up a caution sign?

After four sons, my one and only daughter arrived. I discovered that girls are different. I expected her interests wouldn't be the same as theirs. Her drawings were filled with self-portraits of little girls in skirts with long lashes, donning shoes and purses. I was used to trucks and jets. But this didn't surprise me. The surprising difference, I didn't notice until she was about four.

I had a one step ladder that I used to change light bulbs. With ladder in one hand and a new bulb in the other, I positioned the ladder under the ceiling fixture. Unknown to me at the time, she had been watching me. Before I could ascend the ladder, she called, "Wait, daddy"! And then she said, "let me hold the ladder for you".

Fear of Lizards

I t is not unusual to be fearful of lizards. Both my wife and sister have herpetophobia. My sister's fear of lizards is legendary amongst the family. In the contemporary phrase, "she freaks out". The term is descriptive, but inadequate. She neither screams nor runs, she freezes. She enters a state of rigidity and silence. The following account is based on my brother-in-law's first-hand observations.

At the time, the following incident occurred, they were living on Fountainbleu Drive near Carrolton Avenue. Apple street ends at Carrolton and resumes as Fountainbleu, a tree lined boulevard with a well-kept median. The neighborhood changes dramatically into more stately homes. One sees no taverns or any business use of space. Many of the homes have basements and the front porches are a story above street level. There are none of the modest doubles one finds on Apple Street. The whole feel of the neighborhood is different. Neither the noise of traffic nor the chatter of people walking about is present. There is more green space and privacy; and no on-street parking. It was in this beautiful New Orleans neighborhood that terror struck.

As my sister backed out of the drive way, she preceded her drive toward Napoleon Avenue and suddenly she froze, unable to speak or move. She was about two blocks from Carrolton Avenue and before long cars began to pile up behind her. As fate would have it, a solitary lizard had decided to sun bath on her windshield. Her hands were clasping the steering wheel and her body was bent over and motionless. I do not know how long she remained in this piteous state, but she was eventually rescued by one inconvenienced driver.

The driver, several cars behind her, got out of his pickup truck to enquire about the jam. When he reached my sister's car and saw her motionless, his concern grew. "Are you okay, ma'am"? Her response was so repressed and weak, he repeated his question. "Are you okay, ma'am"? "What is the matter"? Barely above a whisper my sister replied, "There's a lizard on my car"! So soft was her reply, he asked her to repeat it. "Where's the lizard"? Remaining in her frozen state, she replied, "On the windshield". He bent over to inspect the windshield and with one flick of his finger, he sent the hapless lizard sailing. "Oh, you mean that one; he's gone now". Without further discussion, he walked back to his truck. In a moment, my sister was recomposed and was on her way and so were a score of relieved drivers.

And how do you get a lizard stuck to your windshield? An avowed protector sweeps it there. Concerned that you might encounter a scary lizard, he attacks them with his broom. The dead and dying ones he sweeps off the porch, but one gets stuck to your windshield. His anxiety over your fear doomed his good intentions. Anxiety beats carelessness at breaking dishes.

Lizards by Mail

Have you ever received a surprise in the mail? I bet it was a check, candy or flowers. It wasn't a lizard, was it? One of the rottenest pranks one could do is to send a herpetophobiac a lizard in the mail. What kind of person would do such a thing? Little boys will do it to their mother. My kids did it to their mother, my long-suffering wife.

Technically speaking, they didn't actually box it, stamp it and post it. That would require forethought and money; they had neither. What they actually did was to put numerous lizards through the mail slot in the front door.

I suppose that it was common enough in the 1970s to have mail slots instead of mail boxes. The advantage of a mail slot is that the mail goes safely inside the house. My kids understood that their post would be immediately delivered. Of course, they still had to time their delivery when mother was there to receive her surprise.

Their strategy seems to have been to time delivery to coincide with vacuuming the foyer. They probably gathered by the door when they heard mother practicing her home making skills. I am sure there were muffled giggles and chatter as they anticipated their mother's reaction. She had to know that something was afoot. But they had to stay at the scene of the crime to hear her reaction.

What they heard were screams of terror. What they didn't see was her dance of terror. The next thing they saw and heard was mother as she yelled out. "You come in here and catch every one of these"! And she added, "let me see you take it outside". She watched the solemn procession of rebuked kids try to conceal laughter. "You make sure you get everyone; you hear me"!

I can't say for sure that the lizard she found in the folds of her blouse a week later was one they missed. Neither can I charge that the cold and dead toad left in the refrigerator was a willful act. Also, the toad enclosed in a can of blue playdoh was also probably unplanned. I just don't know for sure. What I do know is that, even today, when a lizard enters the house, she calls for me to get it. I must show her that it is in my hand and she must see me toss it outside.

Causeway Fear

It's reasonable to be afraid of bridges, particularly one like the Causeway that is 24 miles long. Bad things have happened on the span that connects the south and north shores of Lake Pontchartrain. With the appearance of fog, you can expect pile ups and traffic jams. In almost any weather, a vehicle can hit the railing and land in the Lake. Sometimes it's fatal for the occupants. But to a surprising extent, heroic drivers initiate and successfully accomplish rescues.

But accidents need not happen to extend the trip from a half hour to several hours. Wind and heavy rain necessitate convoy crossings. Motorists are required to drive in single file, escorted by the Causeway Police. And then there is the ever-present road hazards that fall on to the roadway. Ladders, furniture and vehicle parts can cause accidents and always cause jams. There are just some things one learns to live with, and traffic delays on the Causeway is but one. But there are times when traffic backs up for no apparent reason and causes no small amount of worry.

My wife and I had a 10 am closing appointment on a refinance loan at a Northshore bank, and the lawyer was late. Bank officials informed us that the lawyer had called to explain his tardiness. It was a one-word excuse, "Causeway." We waited another hour, and he made his appearance with a whopping tale to tell.

Was it an accident, breakdown or road hazard? None of the above. He explained that traffic was moving at a snail pace. A slow-moving vehicle occupying both lanes was forcing drivers to slow as they passed. "When I got to the cause of the delay, it was the craziest thing I've ever seen. Two ladies wearing orange life vests were blocking both lanes and praying their rosaries."

Crimes and Misdemeanors

How do you keep kids healthy, safe and happy? Who knows? Somehow you communicate to them that whatever slop hole they jump into, you will be coming for them. If you mean it, they will eventually get the message. The only advice that I can give is to take courage. No matter how well behaved and smart, the kids will eventually do something stupid.

Not far from home, a merchant advertised his bean bag chairs by placing his biggest bag on the sidewalk near his shop door. Most people, including thieves, would not attempt to steal such a large item of little value, but kids aren't most people.

Number six son and his accomplice decided that they could pull off this caper. Riding by on their dirt bikes, they simply grabbed the thing, in tandem. It must have been a piece of acrobatic prowess. Each clasping the bag with one hand while the other hand steered. They did it, but didn't get far.

The matter wound up in the juvenile court system. It was eventually resolved in a manner favorable to the court, but not to the kids involved. As it turned out, my son's accomplice was well known to the juvenile authorities and his home situation was not good. Both kids were remanded to me. As to the fate of the accomplice, prudence requires that I say nothing.

As to the fate of number six son, his life of crime ended when he came to the conclusion that people who lie and steal cannot be trusted. Eventually, several deployments in the military, fighting fires and dodging scud missiles satisfied his thrill-seeking needs. Fortunately, not all acts of stupidity required resolution by the courts.

What do you do when you see a really cool fishing lure and you have neither money nor stealing skill? You do what every kid is tempted to do, you steal it anyway. You take it out of its container and carefully stuff it in your sock until it reaches your ankle. It's that easy; your hands are now empty and you can walk out of the store above suspicion. You get on your bike and in five minutes you are home. Except, your heart's still beating fast; your pressure is elevated; and you are one scared puppy.

When you return home, you try to retrieve the lure that's safely tucked in your now bloody sock. You need help separating the lure from the ankle and the lure from the sock. Enter dad. After separating the tangle mess and cleaning superficial wounds, I returned number two son and the lure to the store. With some embarrassment on our part and a large amount of good will on the store manager's part, all went well.

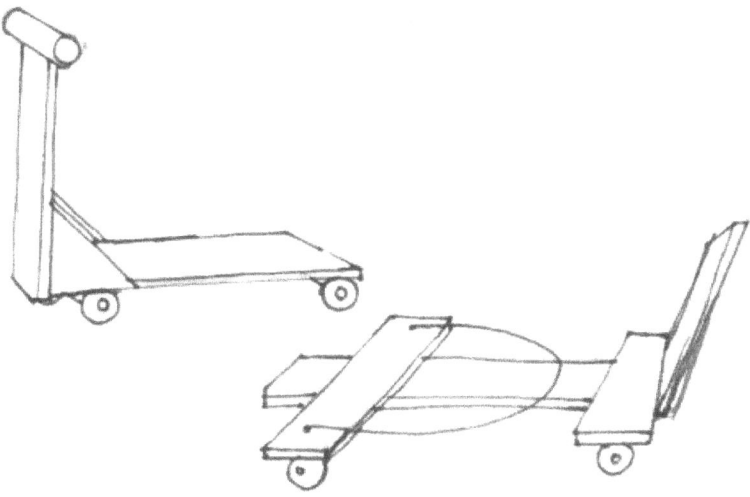

Lost Scout Troop

My earliest recollections are playing in puddles, and then catching creatures in ditches and lagoons. By the time I was old enough to have a knife, cut cane and buy fishing hooks, I was hooked on fishing. When my eight children arrived (one at a time as is customary), it was no surprise to my wife that I would take them along and that at least a few would catch the fishing disease.

I often took several of my children to local fishing holes to catch bream, which in New Orleans are called perch. It took about thirty-five or forty to feed my family. When the kids were young. wary of small bones, I would filet the fish we caught either at Bayou St. John or the back lagoons of City Park. It was in City Park near Scout Island that we were told a troop of boy scouts was lost!

As I recall, only one fishing buddy was with me that day. As we concentrated on fishing, suddenly a boy scout appeared behind us. He engaged us in light conversation about fishing and then, like an unexpected tug on your fishing line, he surprised us. He casually announced that his entire scout troop was lost! It seemed incredible to us that two dozen boy scouts and their scout leaders could simply vanish in the wilds of City Park. I looked at my fishing buddy and we both came to the same conclusion. We picked up our lines and turned from fishing to hunting. "Where did you last see them"? He pointed to a nearby location and we followed his lead. We walked a stone's throw from where we were fishing and heard the chatter of boys. As the source of the chatter passed a clearing in the brush, we caught sight of boys in scout uniforms. How far they had wandered, I do not know. But not one of them revealed the tell-tale signs of having been lost. When our new acquaintance saw his friends, he yelled out to them. It wasn't a voice of relief from dissipating fear, but rather a matter of fact tone. As we faded from the scene, we could discern his words but not their response. "Where were you guys"?

My son and I caught fish that day and that pleased us and our hungry-for-fish family. It was an illuminating experience for me. It takes a great deal of courage and a little self-deception to leave boyhood behind.

They Call Me Pops

I can't remember exactly when I became "pops" to my children. In hindsight, I know that it was an important development. Shakespeare's oft quoted line concerning names and the smell of roses needs qualification; names do matter. Consider the prayer that all Christians usually know from memory. The English translation of the Our Father doesn't quite capture the meaning of the original. The words "pops" or "daddy" are closer to the intended meaning. Imagine what life would be like if we really looked upon God as, "pops".

When my children called me "pops", I knew that my wallet would be lighter or I would be doing something I didn't really want to do. Furthermore, I knew how I would respond to their request. I wasn't going to say "no". It seems to me that there is a big difference between asking "father" for a favor and asking "pops". When a child calls his father "pops", he knows that whatever he requests, he will receive. Now a "father", on the other hand, is carefully approached with some fear and the realization that a request may not be granted. The shift from "father" to "pops" signals a shift in a relationship from fear to trust and from distant to close.

I fancy that all good fathers want to be "pops" to their children. Taking time to talk to children is one way they do it. Far from being uneventful, conversation is often an amusing adventure. You never really know what kids will say. A friend of mine asked his first grader what she learned in catechism class. "We learned all about heaven, hell, and suppositories", she declared.

Once while driving granddaughters to Audubon Zoo, one granddaughter expressed her distress over the heat. The ac in our auto was not working and we were all uncomfortable. One granddaughter, expressing her discomfort, declared, "I'm comatose". Another responded, "I'm blueberry toast". Which prompted, "I'm strawberry toast". It went down-hill from there all the way to the Zoo. I believe that five-year-old children use more words than they actually know.

Consider this poetic gem, I first heard my firstborn son recite when he was about seven, "Boys go to Mars and get candy bars. Girls go to Jupiter and get more stupider". It's not original, but it does capture those fleeting conversations I have had with children. Ask a little boy how he feels about girls and he will say, "Girls are stupid". Ask a little girl how she feels about boys and she will say, "Boys are dirty and nasty". This attitude is not a mimic of mother's attitude; it is heart-felt.

But sometimes kids sound like grown-ups. Once I was walking behind a couple of first graders on their way to school and one said, "Why does life have to be so hard"? Similarly, when my four-year-old granddaughter was tired of playing, she abruptly stopped. Casting a glance at everyone in the room, she announced, "I'm really tired. I'm going to bed and nobody bother me". When she was five, she claimed she was six. Thinking that our memory was faulty, we asked her older sister for clarification. Her sister said, "She's a sophisticated five".

In Their Eyes

One of the more challenging tasks a parent faces is to distribute candy justly to children. The more children one has, the more daunting the job. With eight hungry birds with beaks agape waiting for sweet justice, the duty was sometimes beyond my feeble abilities. With one eye on the cost and the other on equitable distribution, I took to counting out M & Ms.

My approach was to buy an industrial size bag and count out eight equal piles, but only after I grabbed a handful to sample. I could always count on some inequality in the piles. It was usually necessary to eat a few more to ensure that the piles would be equal and divisible by eight.

My most persistent anxiety centered not only on the accuracy of my count, but on my children's notion of a broader standard of justice as well. Sometimes, although certain of my addition, I would be overcome by a disquieting thought. What if one says, "He's got more red ones"?

As soon as the candy was distributed and no complaints of injustice were leveled, my anxiety evaporated. But then there were those times that trouble followed fear. Trouble is when some have candy and some don't. The improvident eat with abandonment, the prudent stretch it out. The younger children would wolf it down. The older siblings understood that when it was gone; it was gone.

One day, two of the youngest came to me and complained that an older brother would not let them into his room. Curious as to why he had locked the door, I gently knocked and inquired about the goings-on. He opened the door and asked if I would lock the door behind myself. "Your little brothers want to play in your room", I told him. I missed the whole point. "They want some of my M & M's", he said.

"They keep knocking on my door and asking for candy". My response was simple and just. I boldly declared, "Everyone received the same amount and you should not feel bad if they finished theirs before you". "Just tell them no", I added. " I can tell them 'no' as long as I don't have to see them. That's why I locked my door". I didn't understand his explanation. He added, "You see if I don't look in their eyes, I can tell them 'no'. But, if I see their eyes, I give in and they come back for more and pretty soon I have no candy."

For all my careful arithmetic, my scrupulous concern for equity, I didn't anticipate the problems that surround the virtue of compassion. I hoped that my candy rules would teach them prudence and justice. But despite my efforts, some were already learning that compassion nips the wings of justice. And if one insists on the rule of equity, one must not look into their eyes.

Budding Entrepreneurs

When my children were very small, I would buy a large size of peanut M&M's and count them out. I suppose that from these early experiences they learned some values and skills that would be helpful in their candy sales careers. The lessons learned were pivotal in the pursuit of adult careers; beware of constraint of trade agents and don't reveal trade secrets to competitors.

Number two son developed a sweet little business while attending junior high. He purchased blow pops from a local supermarket and sold them at school for a decent profit. Then he discovered that he could make larger profits by purchasing large bags of the product for even larger profits. In fact, he increased sales and profits so dramatically that it drew the attention of the school authorities. I was called to the school office and had to deliver the bad news that his enterprise was out of business. While praising his enterprising spirit, I was informed that it was against school rules to conduct such operations on school grounds. And from this life lesson, number two son adopted a motto straight out of the American Revolution. "Live free or die".

Number five son encountered no limitation of sales. His problem was of his own making. Having tasted some kid's rock candy, he came home singing its praises. His mother told him that rock candy is not only easy to make, but is very cheap, and its flavor and color could be altered.

He and a business partner made a batch of red, strawberry flavored rock candy. They placed the candy in snack bags and off they went to seek fame and fortune. Sales were skyrocketing, requiring almost daily candy making. Then, unexpectedly, sales plummeted. It seems that he and his business partner started bragging around school that they made their candy from scratch. In the process, they gave away the recipe and revealed all of their trade secrets. The lesson they learned was that just as in basketball, you don't share the ball; in business you don't share your trade secrets.

Teaching the Value of Hard Work

Parents feel compelled to teach their children the value of hard work. Personally speaking, I didn't have to, government did it for me. Number five son learned the value of work the day he received his first pay check. He started his career in construction and was payed as a contract laborer. Naturally talented, he soon was given the nickname "tools" by his teenage friends. He learned a great deal from some talented carpenters and pretty soon he was earning a higher salary than a typical wage laborer. He was an independent subcontractor, but didn't know it. He had none of the many safety nets wage workers enjoy. All he knew was that when he worked over time, he got real cash.

In the construction trades, many laborers are independent contract workers and there are good reasons why. Several incentives encourage employers in the construction trades to treat laborers as independent subcontractors. The turnover rate is very high and the onerous tasks of managing workers is costly and inefficient. An employee requires workers compensation, payroll deductions, medical insurance and retirement benefits. These are just part of the ensemble faced by contractors that encourage them to find another way to do business.

Until he was valuable enough to be a full-time employee, number five son was just a teenager working weekdays to have fun on the weekend. This changed when he became an employee.

I remember him examining his first paystub, "What's up with this"? Noting the difference between gross and net pay, he read off the list of filthy things that forced his hopes and dreams to go south. "Dang, all these taxes"! Then he really got into it. He went into a tirade and became the victim of a universal conspiracy. "That's what's wrong with this world; we hard-working people have to support all those lazy people"! Or spoke similar words to that effect. Overnight, as it were, he turned solid citizen at the ripe age of seventeen.

I Played Santa

Playing Santa was a memorable experience and a big disappointment. Everyone should try it at least one season. My wife's response to me applying for a job to play Santa at a local mall was immediate and positive. We needed the money to buy Christmas presents for our children and, as an Associate Professor at UNO, I had the time during the Christmas break. I had no idea that I was violating University rules.

LSU System rules forbid outside employment, unless that employment is related to your work as teaching and scholarship. An art teacher can create art for sale, and a sociologist can be gainfully employed as a sociologist. The key is that the gainful employment must enhance the goals of the University or one's profession. A trip to France as a visiting professor is the kind of outside employment the guidance has in mind. To be in good standing, all I needed to do was deliver a professional paper on the sociological implications of this that or the other. This, I would have done had not the local actors' union exerted control over the job. But for one glorious Christmas tide, I was Santa.

And what fun it was. I saw so many hopeful children to satisfy Santa for a lifetime. Strangely though, my own children were a bit reluctant. You suppose I looked too familiar to be the real Santa? In any event, for the most part, it was an amusing experience, and in one instance, hilarious. A childless couple approached, or should I say, the woman approached me and asked if her fiancé could sit on my lap and have his picture taken. Santa doesn't refuse heartfelt requests, but the gentleman didn't go for it. "That man is going to think I'm queer or something", he countered her demands. As I recall, he gave in to her request after repeated protestations. But the most memorable encounter was with a beautiful not-so-little girl.

I believe she told me she was nine. She looked like a princess and was dressed like one. Her blond hair fell on her shoulders in curly lusters and draped the hand embroidery of her tailored blue dress. Her blue eyes were as soft as her pleasant smile. Her polite manners and poise betokened a young girl of no small amount of breeding. "And what do you wish for Christmas?", I asked. Her response made me lose my Santa persona.

This angel looked at me and said with the thickest country accent I have ever heard, "I want one of 'dem four-ten shotguns just like my cousin Zeke." Well, so much for first impressions.

Stretching the Limits of Grandfathers

Grandfathers should avoid some activities. Even if they are fun. I know all the baloney imparted by the tired clichés. "You are only as young as you feel". And how about, "You are as young as you think you are"? To all the "young at heart" over 70, pay no attention to that propaganda. There are real limits on the aged. Forget that propaganda or you will pay the price. But most of the time, it's worth the price.

You may recall from a previous snippet that I caught snakes for fun and profit. I taught my children the art of snake catching and it is only reasonable that I should teach my grandchildren.

I have a peculiar habit of showing off by catching snakes without using a snake stick. The technique is simple in theory. As you approach the snake, it flees. You bend down, grasp it by the tail (snakes are slow) and in one smooth movement, you pull it toward your parted legs. The snake is disoriented and confused. While it remains in a state of confusion, you hold the snake's body still by holding your legs together. You pull the snake through your legs until you are able to grasp the snake in your hand. This is a great way to impress grandchildren. You need not tell them that snake hunters simply grab the snake and place it in a pillow case.

One day, in my grandson's backward. I saw a ribbon snake, the kind most commonly seen in gardens. It presented a chance for me to impress him. "I am going to catch this snake for you", I declared. And indeed, I did catch the snake. But because my body didn't move as fast as when I was 18, I allowed the snake to reach the fence and the Cherokee rose vines. Now, Cherokee roses are beautiful. but painful. Their white blossoms can be seen on top of tall pines. Its thorns discourage meddling. I allowed myself to be trapped. I had the snake in my hand, but. I was also caught in a tangle of vines. How do I keep the snake and use both hands to extricate myself? There was only one solution. I had to throw the snake behind me and clear myself of vines and then catch the snake again. It worked! Catching the snake again was not hard, but I wound up in the same predicament, caressed by Cherokee roses. Would the strategy work again? Almost. But the snake disappeared among the vines. As I brushed off my clothes and investigated thorn wounds, Philip's silent disappointment spoke volumes. "Well, would you like for me to show you how I catch mosquito hawks (dragon flies)"?

Forbidden Words

When number seven son was about five, he confided in me about a word one of his brothers used. "Daddy! Daddy! Chuck said the "D" word"! I racked my brains but could not fathom his meaning. I quickly searched my personal lexicon for "D" words. The first word I found, and the most likely candidate, was the word damn. But the sound of the spoken word dam is identical to the forbidden word, damn. Is it possible that his brother said dam but he mistook it for the word, damn? "Son, do you mean that he said damn? Impatient with me, he said, "No! No! The "D" word"! His meaning was as clear as the muddy Mississippi. "You know, the "D" word"! He was getting increasingly agitated and I increasingly perplexed. I reached deeper into my brain and came up empty. I gave him permission to say the forbidden word. "You know, the "D" word, D-I-A-R-R-H-E-A".

Why would he think diarrhea is a forbidden word? And then the answer came to me. Little boys find bathroom talk funny, but mothers do not. Being the youngest, he was probably subjected to more correction than most kids. I don't know if this theory will fly, but all the little boys I have known seem to be fond of talking about poo. Tell them that someone has poo on his shoe and they break into laughter. Dads sometimes encourage such talk in small children, but it is always taboo for mothers. I think I have stumbled upon something very important, but I don't know exactly what. What I do know is that children under five are likely to be confused by the injunction against forbidden words. There is a joke that has traveled the world that illustrates my point.

Two brothers were in serious conversation and the seven-year-old tells the five-year-old, "I'm going to say an ugly word". "I'm going to say, damn". He asks his little brother, "What you gonna say"? Little brother shrugs his shoulders and says, "I don't know". They both sit down for breakfast. Mother asks the older child, "What would you like for breakfast"? He answers, "I'll take some of those damn cherrioes". Mother explodes in anger. She slaps his behind and yells, "Go back to bed you filthy mouth kid"! Still angry, she turns to his little brother and sternly asks, "And WHAT do you want"? The little one sinks into deep thought and after a few moments, he declares, "I don't know. but you can bet your sweet ass it ain't any of those damn cherrioes".

A Funny Thing Happened on the Way to a Funeral

Death is no laughing matter. It's always terrible for the bereaved, but not necessarily for the person lost to them. For many, death can be welcomed relief from pain and suffering. Chesterton once remarked that God has hidden His mirth. Is his mirth too terrible to contemplate? I think not. If human reason is a reflection of the divine, so is humor. Anyway, I don't need much justification for laughing.

Some time ago, a brother of mine was standing next to his father-in-law's coffin. One of the priests in attendance engaged him in small talk. "How is the family? He responded, "Everyone is fine". Pointing to the coffin, he added, "Everyone except Francis here". Even in death, the dead look fine, thanks to morticians' art.

I was always intrigued by mortician's ability to make the dearly departed look life like. For years I tried to fine a remedy for fungal toes. After finally finding a real remedy and faithfully using it, I was amazed at how healthy my toes looked. In fact, I commented to my wife how pleased I was. "I think I am going to instruct the mortician to reverse my body in the coffin so that the bereaved can view my feet". I can only imagine what would be said. "How glad we are that we don't have to view his face". Of course, not everywhere is the wake a custom, but everywhere people like to say their last goodbye before death.

Among Sicilian peasants it is very important for all family members to say their last goodbye. So important, that they use a time-honored technique of estimating the time of death. When the very ill experience a drop in feet temperature, death is only hours away. All family members are told to come in haste. It doesn't always work. My mother told me that when one old immigrant was near death, a family member reached under the covers to feel her feet. At once, she awoke from her coma, sat up and said, "This is not the hour". It is remarkable that some people know when they are going to die and; some say the dying can even postpone death.

Some time ago, I came across a statistical study that claimed that some people, particularly famous people, can postpone death. One example offered was Thomas Jefferson. Near death, Jefferson awoke from his coma and asked, "What day is it"? He was informed that it was not July the fourth. Apparently, he did this more than once until the fourth of July, whereupon he slipped into a coma and died. If I could choose a death date, it would be April the fourteenth, and leave the IRS to ponder my decision.

"A Wolf Bit Me"

One should never make fun of people with mental disorders; decency and morality require us to extend to everyone the dignity bestowed by God, regardless of one's human condition. However, to make fun of craziness, to draw the suffering in on the "joke", to share in our common humanity blurs the line that separates the so-called "normal" from the "not-so-normal". My oldest brother suffered from schizophrenia. Under most conditions, he was fun loving and out-going with a keen sense of humor. When the disease disrupted normal brain processes, he was suspicious and sullen.

I became my brother's principal caretaker, driving him to receive medical treatment, picking up his prescriptions, and later with the passing of my mother and father, visiting him in a variety of places that care for the mentally disordered.

Once my brother Joe was sent to Charity Hospital after a particularly disturbing psychotic episode. But frenzy has its limits and after a couple of weeks of treatment; he was scheduled to be discharged. Charity Hospital's psychiatric ward enjoyed a good reputation. While some indigent patients were treated there, my impression was that most were from the general population in the surrounding civil parishes. As it turned out, the day I visited my brother, he was eager for me to meet his new friend. I was not surprised for it was his habit to make friends and introduce them to me. The medical condition of Joe's new friend was, however, a big surprise.

Standing in front of me and greeting me with smiles, stood my brother and his toothless friend. No matter how hard I tried, I could not turn my eyes away from the terrible hand wound sported by Joe's friend. Neither wisdom nor sensitivity held my curiosity back. "What happened to your hand"? "A wolf bit me", shot back Joe's new friend. "Where were you"? "On Canal St", he replied. "Dang, you hardly ever see wolves on Canal St.", I said as all three of us were enveloped in abiding laughter. And for a moment sanity was summoned from its slumber.

In time, age and the effects of the medicines Joe was taking sent him to the hospital with kidney and heart problems. Soon afterwards, I was told that it was unlikely he would ever be able to care for himself. Thereafter, he resided in a variety of nursing homes and other institutions. His stays in each were cut short when one or more health workers complained that they were afraid of him. Just about everywhere he stayed there was a fear of violence, but not one incidence of violence was ever reported to me. Each forced move would take him further and further away from our old neighborhood. His last stint was in a Baker, Louisiana nursing home, although farther away, it was pleasant place.

It was a sad situation, one that could easily evoke depression in caregivers. But even in the midst of sorrow laughter does not sleep long. Earlier, visiting Joe at an institution on Chef Menteur Highway, he called me to the side, motioning me to keep quiet and spoke in Italian. "Please, speak Italian; these people know all my business"! "Look Tony, we got to have a signal so they won't know when you are coming". "Okay, Joe what's it gonna be"? "Alright, when you arrive, I want you to beep your horn fourteen times"! I convulsed into laughter and then I said, "Joe that will fool the hell out of them"! Joe did show signs of indignation, but I fancy that I saw a tiny smile enter the scene and showed itself on his lips and in his eyes.

Recognizing Really Bad Ideas

As part of my attempt to deal with one auto family issues and an abiding fondness for walking, I would frequently walk all or part of the way home from work. I have no idea how far it is from the University of New Orleans and Bucktown. (formerly a fishing village on Lake Ponchartrain and now just another suburban neighborhood).

It is a nice enough walk down Robert E. Lee Boulevard pass City Park to the south and the pleasant homes of Lake Vista to the north. But suddenly the orderly world of neat houses and the tranquility of City Park's lagoons give way to a tangle of streets as Robert E. Lee crosses Ponchartrain Boulevard. Only the broad neutral ground (median) gives you a clue that you are passing over a former navigational channel that once served as water passage from the Lake to the back side of the French Quarter. Once passed this point you are only three blocks from the Seventeenth Street Canal and an impressive concentration of seafood restaurants. The aromas of seafood frying and crabs boiling always made me hasten my steps to home and supper.

Now, I say it is a pleasant enough walk when the air is cool and crisp as it generally is in October. But, for most of the year, the air is wet and uncomfortable. In the summer, the heat and humidity paralyze the brain. Well, that's the best excuse I can invent for my uncritical acceptance of a really off-the-wall idea.

One particularly hot and humid July as I was passing the lagoons of City Park, I noticed workers were clearing out the water hyacinths. I fished the bayous of Louisiana and know that streams even ones with strong tidal movement get congested by this most beautiful pest. For a non-flow lagoon, the build-up is quick and deadly to aquatic life.

Workers were using heavy equipment to lift knots of hyacinths, placing them in five-foot mounds on the banks.

Someone else was watching the same scene. A plumber standing beside his van was shaking his head in disapproval as he watched the growing mounds of vegetation. His gaze still fixed on the removal of the hyacinths; he expressed his feelings emphatically "Look at that! What a shame! Look at all that good vegetation going to waste! Why don't they put the hippos from Audubon Zoo in the lagoons so they can eat it?" I paused only long enough to agree with him before I continued on my way.

I am sure most people would think that transporting hungry hippos across town so they can feast on the abundant vegetation in City Park is a bad idea. However, it took me a few minutes to realize that I just agreed with a lunatic. In my defense, I submit as evidence of my sanity that it was July and it was hot.

Where is Nguyen?

I am not sure when my university classes became peopled with older students, but it did improve class room discussions. After a class presentation on attitudes toward death in modern and traditional societies, one mature student approached the podium. She wanted to underscore her agreement with the idea that traditionalists view death as part of nature. The closer a person is to nature, the more inclined they are to accept death as the price for life. After agreeing with the point of the lecture, she continued to augment her agreement. I was always, more or less, prepared for student response, but I was not prepared for the story she would tell.

As faithful to her account as I can remember, she described what happened one day with the yard crew in Jefferson Parish. With so many medians and canal banks in the Parish, a number of crews are set to cut the grass and weeds. A supervisor drops off a score of workers at a designated intersection in the morning. By mid-afternoon, they are expected to finish the scheduled work, clean their tools and wait for the supervisor to transport them back to the warehouse.

After the fall of Saigon, many Vietnamese immigrants arrived in the area. As skilled agriculturalists, many were hired to maintain the medians and canal banks in Jefferson Parish.

One day, as the story was reported to me by the aforementioned student, a rather extraordinary thing happened. While working the canal bank, an all Vietnamese crew experienced the death of a crew member. A very old and sickly immigrant died while working. One can only imagine what the scene would be like had it happened to a non-immigrant. Ambulances, fire trucks and police cruisers would have filled the intersection and attracted scores of on lookers. Traffic would have come to a stop. But nothing of the sort happened. Passers-by did not even take notice. Instead of nervous chatter, the scene was as peaceful as a pasture of grazing cattle. Using their garden tools, they interred old Nguyen right where he died, after a brief ceremony.

When the supervisor arrived for the return trip, he did not suspect a thing until after the head count. When he realized the count was one less than it should have been, he questioned the workers. "Where is Nguyen?" One worker explained that Nguyen was very old and very sick. "No family, it is good that Nguyen is gone." Then it hit the supervisor. "O my God! Where is Nguyen?"

The bell sounded, warning me that I was late for my next class. I never did hear the rest of the story, but I can imagine that there was more commotion over Nguyen's exhumation than over his death.

Teaching

I taught at the University of New Orleans for over thirty years and was also in the first graduating class. I have many fond recollections of dedicated teachers and colleagues. I even boast that I knew a couple of saints who poured themselves out for the benefit of their students. But most colleagues I knew were a lot like me, sons and daughters of Adam and Eve. Most enjoyed teaching, but on occasion could bring themselves to voice criticism of the bureaucracy and students. Once, I was part of a complaining party, when several colleagues condemned students for their lack of intelligence and work ethic. Others chimed in agreement. I couldn't restrain myself and yelled out, "This would be a great place to work if there were no students."

While I have many fond recollections, I can recall two in particular that stand out. A standing ovation is hard to forget and so is a death threat. The standing ovation came when I was assigned or I should say volunteered to teach a large class of students who were remedial in both math and English. The attrition rate was over ninety percent for our least prepared students. Using federal grant money, the University launched a special program to help retain the least prepared students. The plan was to offer a program of instruction that was laced with help for all the difficulties freshmen encounter. This it would do by presenting more demanding lectures and labs. It was kind of a college within a college. I was asked to teach the sociology. Some of my colleagues gave me a good-natured hard time. "You are going into the zoo", some said.

My first lecture covered the founders of sociology, not exactly exciting stuff. I was determined to do my best. I maintained the same energy level until the bell rang. And there I was standing looking over a sea of students standing, applauding and shouting approval. None of the teaching awards, not even the one that was accompanied by a grand, gave me as much satisfaction. That was the high in teaching, I would also experience a low.

One day I got a telephone call from the Dean, who informed me that a student had threatened to kill me. I told the Dean after he had named the student that I didn't believe that this student would really try to kill me. Nonetheless, I was prepared to face tomorrow. The next class day, I didn't notice anything unusual. Later, I was informed that the police had scurried the student away before she arrived on campus. They had put her into a psychiatric facility. Upon seeing me in the morning the Chair of the Department said, "I see that you haven't been killed yet." My response, as I recall, was "I thought the lecture wasn't particularly good, but I didn't think it was that bad." For a very long time, I wandered what I could have done to help her. And as fate would have it, she came to my office two years later accompanied by a relative. The purpose of her visit was to seek my advice. It was a terrible thing to hear how she felt being locked up as a psychiatric patient. Painful childhood arthritis and the capricious rules of the University conspired to make her life miserable. I recommended that she not take legal action, not because I thought the University blameless, but that to do so might undo the progress she had already made. She took my advice. All is well that ends well.

Monster Patrol

What do you do about monsters in the closet? Do you tell your children that it is silly to believe that monsters are in your closet? I've had to confront this problem several times in the course of raising children. I tried the obvious and told them that there are no such things as monsters. Did they believe me? I tried to approach this problem by imagining that they think logically. I soon learned that the problem is not solvable by logic or any appeal to reason. But monsters in the closet can keep everybody awake for a long night.

I hit upon a solution without any consultation with experts. I decided I should approach it another way. I found that it was fun to play along. In no time, the whole problem turned into a game. With my best acting face on, I went into the closet appearing to be frightened. My three-year old was both frightened and amused. I lingered in the closet and feigned fear, then quickly ran back. I asked, "Did you see that monster? His head looks like a tennis shoe with string beans stuffed in it. Let's go back and look again." Together we approached the closet gingerly. I held his hand and we walked into the closet. "Oh no! There are two monsters in the closet. And both are ugly and funny." He laughed. I laughed. We both laughed, then I said, "let's look under the bed."

We approached the bed very carefully. Then I said, "Oh no, there's one here too. And he's the funniest thing I ever saw in my life. He has a long nose and floppy ears. He is pink with blue polka dots." By this time, we were both laughing and having a great deal of fun. What logic was incapable of curing, imagination shooed away.

Much later I learned that this approach is the one recommended by experts. It requires some acting ability, which not everyone has. Once I convinced a student to try it. Her three-year-old daughter kept her up at night fearful of the monsters in her closet. I told her about monster therapy and I thought that she might want to try it. She did exactly as I recommended. When she returned to class, she told me how the therapy went. She said that her daughter was unimpressed by her acting ability. Apparently, my student was so bad at acting that she bored her poor child to death. Really irritated by her mother's performance, little Melissa said, "Mother you look ridiculous." From that time on, Melissa never mentioned monsters again.

To tell your child that there are no such things as monsters simply does not work. Not only that, it is in one sense a lie. Grown-ups do believe in monsters, but not the kind that scare children. Grown-ups are afraid of "real" monsters. Are my body parts the perfect size and shape? Am I really getting wrinkles? Do I have enough money? Do I really have all the things that my neighbors have? These are the monsters, and many others, that keep grown-ups awake at night. So, don't tell children that there are no monsters in the closet. Instead, try telling them that your monsters are reasonable, but there's are not?

Too Many Words

What do you do when you use too many words? Do you patiently accept the results and continue your old ways? Or, do you change and embrace a life of brevity? I take insults well and then prepare for the worst. When I prolong a comment or summon a long answer to a short question, my wife will shout out, TMW, before I finish. The end result is only a little amusement for people listening. But in the classroom, almost anything can happen.

Despite the fact that the university mandates a written explanation of grading systems, you still must orally explain what it takes to earn a letter grade. I would always start off with an explanation of how one earns a C grade. Invariably, a student would call out, "how about a B"? I would say you need 240 points or more to make a B. Anticipating the next question, "For an A, you need to attach your request to a $100 bill ". The bell rang and the students departed. As they made a mad dash for the door, one student lingered. He approached me and casting his gaze from side to side, he broached a question for which I was not prepared. Still circumspect in demeanor, he quietly said, "how much money did you say?" I looked at him and said, "you didn't say that and I didn't hear it."

Too many words can cause problems, If only a momentary uneasiness. There was an incident when gratuitous words caused trouble for many for at least a week. It was the second to last class before the fall break and I was fired up and on a roll. Pearls of knowledge fell from my lips and wishing to curb demagogic excess, I said something I would later regret. "If this gets good, I want you to pass the basket".

On the last day of class I saw something unusual. I noticed two or three students out of place. Then, I noticed that a basket was being passed. Being only a part-time genius, I didn't make a connection until they finished. Then, the bell rang and students handed me a basket with some money and lots of pieces of paper, on which was written "IOU ".

When I got to my office, I counted out $57.36 "Oh my God, what do I do now"? I walked down the hall and asked the Chair of my Department for advice. He laughed and said, "I don't know, but I'll ask the Dean ". The Dean didn't know, so he sent the problem up the chain of command. When it got to the Chancellor's Office, they ask for direction from the LSU System. Several days later, I got the results of my query. "You won't believe what you have to do according to system rules. To avoid a bureaucratic nightmare, the Dean's advice is to spend it ". So, I spent it and I don't remember on what. After all, I delivered some excellent lectures and the worker deserves his pay. I may well have thought of other justifications for my decision.

Neatness Counts

I always knew that my wife practiced heroic virtue. She was and is a very neat person. I am somewhat challenged in this regard. She suspected that my office was a disaster zone but, did not believe that a wife should visit her husband's workplace. She thought it unseemly for a woman to do so. She instructed our only daughter to be her proxy.

As the Sicilians say, "The cat's daughter either bites or scratches". She neither bites nor scratches, but she is organized and has perfected her house keeping skills. As I recall, my daughter was around 13 or so, but had a keen eye for detecting disorder and the management skills to eradicate it.

I believe she received special instructions from my wife. There is no question that she got her DNA from her mother, including an absolute intolerance of dirt and disorder. In no time, my magnificent neglect began to disappear. One after one, items were removed from my desk that I would not see again. Before she trashed an item, she would hold it in front of me. "Do you need this"? When I said no or hesitated, she would trash it. Every item on my desk was either saved or not saved. It disturbed me that she would not tolerate a "maybe" category. When she finished the desk, she started on the wall of books.

She began again to create two categories of books, saved and trashed. I found it hard to part with old text books, even though I no longer used them. My desk and file draws suffered a similar fate. Relentlessly, she made me make these heart-rending decisions. And when her work was done and my agony lessened, I had the cleanest and neatest office at the University. I thanked her and we departed for home.

When we arrived home, she gave her mother a full report. I was not privileged to hear it, because it was not for my ears. I put two and two together and concluded that it was decided that dad is a hopeless case. Shortly after the "big clean", I received a present from my wife. It was a desk ornament. I thought it odd that she would add to my desk clutter. But after staring at the gift, I understood. It read, "Creative Minds Are Often Untidy".

A Wife's Hyperbole

I read somewhere that hyperbole is an essential tool in constructing humor. It always tickled me, especially when it was beyond the pale and unexpected. I always associated it with country folks. I still get a laugh from my father-in-law's one liners, even though he is no longer around to deliver them in person. "Listen, if I tell you that a rooster can pull a plough, hitch him up." My favorite is, "that fella is so crooked that when he dies, they won't bury him, they'll screw him into the ground."

My wife grew up in that country milieu, but she didn't use it to get a laugh. It was her customary clichés used for emphasis. It would get a laugh out of me when she would tell one of our children, "If you don't stop what you are doing, I'm going to knock you into next month".

I remember once I did something really dumb and she was perturbed. She looked at me and said, "I love you, but I am still going to hit you with this cane". And then there were those between a rock and a hard place statements.

"I need something decent to wear, but I don't have any clothes to go shopping". I got the message; I would counter with, "Well, I'm too sick to go to the doctor". And then she would say, "I need to go to the beauty parlor, but I can't go anywhere with my hair looking like this". "Yeh. I know what to do, but I can't find the time to improve my time management skills".

When we got tired of listening to both other people's complaints and our own, we tried to steer away from the dark side by exaggerating our aches. I would say, "My arthritis is killing me". She would counter, "Your pains are nothing, mine are much more painful than yours".

Then, she would add, "listen, it is all about me". I would rebel. "Unfair! Unfair"! Then she would say, "It's my turn to complain, it's your job to listen and shut up". I never could win these games.

Whenever I left town to attend a sociological convention or gave a speech to a local organization, she was ready with her homespun advice. She would say something to prevent my head from swelling. Something like, "Take your medicine and don't bother anybody".

The Book I Never Wrote

While in a serious discussion with my wife, I popped the question. "Sand, I am thinking about writing a book connecting the name of a person with his or her occupation. "What are you talking about"? Then, I preceded to tell her that while researching animal aggression, I came across a book entitled "Animal Behavior". The authors are Tiger and Foxx, I told her. "You made that up". she said. I flatly denied the accusation and offered a few other examples of my sincerity. I invited her and the reader to feel free to check my claims. There once was a Cardinal from the Philippines whose name was Cardinale Sin. Immediately, she responded, "You made that up too". "I suppose you don't believe that there was a Southern Baptist radio preacher by the name of Joe Lovelady"? "Listen, nobody can make that up. Truth is stranger than fiction". I tried to convince her that I was serious.

"With some serious research, you and I could write a book about the connection between a person's name and occupation". It took me awhile, but I finally got her attention. "I can think of many more examples", I said. "Surly you thought of that ever popular standby, the psychiatrist named Dr. McNutt".

She still was not convinced, so I challenged her again to use the internet and check my facts. I knew she wouldn't bother with such trivia, so I decided to hit her with one more example. "Would you believe there are several past and present dentists named Dr. Payne? I wonder if people are afraid of going to a dentist whose name is Dr. Payne"? "I have a problem going to the dentist, regardless of his or her name", she said. "Well, don't you think I am on to something here"? "Yes". She said. "You ought to pursue this, but count me out".

Sad to say, I didn't write it. Yet, to paraphrase G.K. Chesterton, I never wrote this book. But of all the books I never wrote, it is by far the best book I have never written.

Naming and Renaming

I am thankful that I lived on Apple Street when I was in grade school. I shudder when I think of the poor children who lived on Tchoupitoulas Street. By the time a kindergartener learns to spell Tchoupitioulas, he's in college. The committees in charge of naming streets have no regard for small children struggling to please their teachers. Consider a small child writing "Oretha Castle Haley Boulevard". He could miss recess. Yes, I am grateful that I lived on Apple Street. When I reflect on the subject, it makes me think of naming and renaming, from streets to cities.

I can't remember when St. Petersburg became Petrograd. I don't even know when "El Pueblo de Neustra Senora La Reina de Los Angeles" (the village of our Lady Queen of the Angels) became the City of Los Angeles. I don't know much about these matters, but historians do. Unfortunately, historians put that information in books in a place they call a library. However, I do know about some recent events that speak loudly about how important changing names can be.

Recently, the authorities of San Francisco met to address a serious problem. Their stated purpose was to decide on when schools would reopen safely after the pandemic. Anxious parents and children awaited their announcement. However, renaming schools is so important that it took precedence over school opening issues. While the authorities did not come to a consensus on reopening schools, they did make substantial progress in renaming several schools. While the country debates the appropriateness of school name changes, my concerns lay elsewhere.

What do you do with apparel that bears the logos of cancelled school names? No one to my knowledge has broached this issue. Is there a final resting place for the once treasured items? Are they to be rudely dispatched without ceremony or honor? Are we to be left pointing to the dumpster sorrowfully declaring, "There lies my daughters Jefferson High School jacket." Who will mourn with me?

Word Combinations and Cliches

Nothing can be more destructive of mental health and tranquility than the mindless repetition of cliches. However, at the hands of the linguistically challenged, they can be funny. A former Mayor of New Orleans has been quoted saying, "And that's the way the cookie bounces." That same mayor wanted to quell rumors during Hurricane Betsy and said, "Don't believe any rumors, unless you hear them from me." But generally speaking, rigid word combinations are annoying. The reasonable combination "sooner or later" can quickly become a nightmare when someone cleverly changes it.

I can't remember when I first heard it, but President Clinton was fond of saying "sooner rather than later". Thereafter, scores of politicians were repeating it. Not long after, you could not watch the news without hearing, "At the end of the day". If that wasn't enough to depress a healthy mind, the crafters are now trying to alter reality.

I thought it odd during the Vietnam conflict that the military referred to bombing of villages as "protective aerial strikes against indigenous populations". But the problem has only worsened. Euphemisms have become so common that it has become difficult to tell whether they arise from an Ivy League professor or a bard at the local bar. A street drug dealer has been called an "undocumented pharmacist". Which is, of course, a response to "undocumented migrants". How far should one go to spare another's feelings? I have a suspicion that the push to correct the linguistically challenged has more to do with manipulation than concern for feelings. And then came the attack on pronouns.

Watch your pronouns, or better yet, deep-six them. In the beginning was the word, but now so many words are off limits. I thought it was a nice gesture to use "his or hers" as an expression of solidarity with women's rights. But the situation has become intolerable. All binary language is an affront to some. All languages that have male, female and neuter nouns are out of luck. But it's not only words that are under the thumb of the communication police; gestures have also come under scrutiny.

Don't clap and risk being branded insensitive to the hearing impaired. But if I use my two index fingers to clap, am I not being cruel to the visually impaired? Is it really fair for me to enjoy peanuts, while others are denied this pleasure because of their allergy? Should I eat a hamburger knowing that animal rights advocates and vegetarians will think I lack virtue? Do I reframe from eating because someone somewhere is hungry? How do I preserve my moral integrity in the face of conflicting moral authorities?

What to cook. what to cook. what to cook?

Backstage Performances

Despite its share of naval gazing, sociology has produced some enduring gems. Ervin Goffman's analysis of everyday interactions is among the best. In all relationships, you want others to think the best of you. To accomplish this, you put your best foot forward and hide the rest.

As a young teacher of sociology, I developed my own strategy to present myself in a favorable light; and when I didn't, I did my best to conceal what I didn't wish to reveal. However, no matter how much you prepare, backstage performances happen. Sadly, a momentary lapse of poise, loss of thought or words can discredit an otherwise sound lecture, leaving the students to doubt whether you are a teacher.

My Sicilian heritage, with its theatric flare served me well as a teacher. The fact that I smoke a pipe, a prop that encouraged students to accept the claim to knowledge, was also very helpful. Armed with these and a love of teaching helped me to earn a reputation as a good lecturer. However, there were times when things didn't go well.

Once, in a large auditorium filled with more than two hundred students, I bagged the mother of all backstage intrusions. I stood on an elevated stage, a podium holding about an inch of lecture notes was in front of me, and a chalkboard behind. I began the lecture with gusto, holding a piece of chalk and an eraser in my right hand, I spun around to begin writing. I hit the chalkboard with such force that both chalk and eraser went flying into the assembly of students. As fate would have it, my circular momentum carried me toward the podium, and my right hand struck it, scattering my lecture notes across the stage. Incredibly, at that precise moment, my clip-on tie fell off. The entire class burst into incurable laughter.

After the laughter subsided and I had regained my composure, I continued to the conclusion of the lecture. I am positive that not one student remembered that lecture. I am equally sure that all remember the backstage performance.

More Backstage

There is good reason why actors practice their lines. Overcome by forgetfulness, performers must ad lib, and unless done with finesse, the entire performance is discredited. I once witnessed a history teacher writing out the difficult words he would use in his lecture. He didn't dare misspell a word on the blackboard. Only later would I discover the wisdom of his actions. It's quite understandable to forget the spelling of foreign place names and people, but simple English words is another matter.

Once I was writing on the blackboard and came to a full stop. I could not remember how to spell the word, "THIN"! I was forced to elicit help from the class. I recovered from my embarrassment and continued the lecture. But there were times when I was forced to exit, "stage right."

I was teaching an elementary statistics class to very fearful students. I told them that the calculation was so easy that anyone could do it. I wrote the numbers used to compute the statistic on the blackboard to demonstrate the procedure. Suddenly, I came done with amnesia. I couldn't even begin.

Honesty is the best policy, but here it was the only policy. What could I do to restore their confidence in my ability? I dismissed the class and promised that I would teach them to compute the statistic as soon as I learned it myself. It wouldn't have been so bad an experience had I not waxed on about how simple the computation was. It was the gratuitous words that caused the problem, or at least exacerbated it. Unnecessary words in my lectures were always getting me onto the backstage. Once, I told my class that "If this (lecture) gets good, pass the basket." But that's a snippet for another day.

No Respect

As a young college graduate awaiting to start my graduate studies, I had some time on my hands. A friend of mine convinced me that we should visit the Catholic Worker house of hospitality in New York City. Started by a very dedicated women, Dorothy Day, the house of hospitality was located in the Bowery, an area known for its poor and homeless population. One could get a free meal there and some respite from the noise and craziness of the streets. The idea was to reproduce in America, the houses of hospitality of Medieval Europe. It's co-founder, Peter Maurin was steeped in Catholic piety and critical of contemporary Christians. He wrote, and I paraphrase, In the first century, Christians would clothe, feed and shelter the poor at their own expense. And the pagans would say, "See how they love one another". Today, government takes care of the poor; and the pagans say, "See how they pass the buck".

Driven by my youthful idealism, I took a train to New York to investigate. I went alone, my friend couldn't make it. The long coach ride took a full day to reach the City. I sheltered down at the local Salvation Army flop house, before I arrived to help in the soup kitchen. The night that I spent at the Salvation Army flop house was a lesson on respect, or maybe disrespect. In any event, it was a bargain.

Like most buildings in New York, it was a tall building. I was offered a room for 50 cents a night, or 75 cents if I wanted a room with a window. I chose a room with a window, from which I could see the bricks of the adjacent building. No alcohol was permitted. I was tired after the train ride and fell asleep immediately. At around 2 am, I was awakened by loud noises. I got up to investigate the matter; I opened my door and discovered the source of the commotion.

Down the hall were several police officers wrestling an intoxicated man from his room and dragging him to the elevator. I was so sound asleep I didn't hear the psychotic episode (delirious tremors) that prompted the call to the police. I was told that he saw bugs and terrible things on his person and was screaming for help, which prompted other guests to hollow at him to shut up.

The last noise I heard was the sound of someone thrown into the elevator accompanied by the chatter of police officers. I don't recall going back to sleep, but I do remember being glad to see the first light of morning. The lesson that I learned that night was that intoxication gets one no respect. I was eager to see what would transpire in the morning at the soup kitchen.

What is Respect?

Standing on the sidewalk in front of the house of hospitality, I was soaking in the sights and sounds of the Big Apple. My appetite having been satisfied by a decent meal, I paused for a smoke. I thought it wise to dispense with store bought cigarettes. I bought some Bull Durham, to roll my own cigs. I recalled being warned that the streets were not safe and not to bring any valuables. Since I had no valuables, it was eazy to comply. I was particularly warned about very dangerous characters that live on the streets. I encountered many interesting people but no dangerous ones. However, after puffing away on a poorly crafted cigarette, I saw two homeless men walking toward me. I remembered the warnings and was cautious. They were a strange pair. Both were clearly indigents dressed in old ill-fitting clothes. One was simply staring in space while the other held his hand and directed his steps. Maybe these two are what they referenced as characters to be wary of. About five feet before they reached me, they stopped and the one in charge stared at my cigarette. "O Boy, what are they up to"? I thought to myself. The one being led was silent, rigid and stared into empty space. The other politely asked for a cigarette. I passed my tobacco to him, but dropped the paper. Instinctively, I said, "Excuse me". I picked up the paper and handed it to him. In a moment, he rolled out the best-looking hand rolled cigarette I had ever seen. I lit it for him and he took a deep draw and placed it in the lips of his friend to take a draw. He asked for another cigarette for his friend, who continued to stare into space. The ritual was repeated; he thanked me and began to walk off. I was relieved that they were on their way and felt foolish to think these two would harm me. But suddenly my fear returned and intensified.

They stopped and walked back to where I stood. The conscious one asked a disturbing question. "Do you know what respect is"? I don't recall my feeble answer, but the question disturbed me. He looked me straight into my eyes and I could see the eyes of a person immune to pain. They were tired and emotionless eyes.

My apprehension of this duo redoubled when he asked the question, but his answer to his own question gave me relief. With an expressionless voice and face. "That's what I have for you, respect", he said. He then turned around and led his companion down the street. I tried to make some sense of the moment. On the long trip back home, my thoughts returned to them again and again. Then, it occurred to me that in this world, we fuss over the king but we give bums the rush. My politeness was instilled in me until it became habit. But to one that has been given the rush, it must have been a refreshing experience not be brushed away. I had forgotten how important manners are as a sign of respect.

Smartest Person I Know

Time Magazine publishes its' list of smartest people annually. I have generally ignored this time wasting topic, largely because I am never included in anyone's list. There is an important element to this topic that needs to be said, and I am just the person that needs to say it. You can't be an earth dweller and not hear the superlative label attached to a friend or relative. "Uncle Willis is the smartest person I know." And who hasn't heard, "Nobody was as smart as my mother." Is this expected family bias, or is there an element of truth in the claim?

America's got talent and so does the world. And if the United States has more, it's because she has more freedom. Without economic and political restrictions, individuals develop their talents. The best ideas, skills, art and literature can be found in the general population, not the great centers of learning. To be sure, universities house very talented people. I worked the better part of my adult life at univerisities and had the good fortune of knowing some very talented people. Very often, their skills are limited to a very narrow body of knowledge. Outside their sphere of expertise, they rely on stereotypes to flesh out what they know about the world. It is not uncommon to encounter a brilliant scientist who is unable to control his own children. This is not to put down the contributions of talented professors, but it is to say that I was always more impressed by creative individuals outside universities.

The individual who creates something new and pursues an idea to fruition, risking failure, impresses me. The really creative individuals are found in business, or if you prefer, business offers the opportunity for the talented to emerge. The unwise and untalented don't survive. Mediocrity gets you nowhere in business unless fortune smiles on you. But fortune is a strange dame and the wise don't count on her. Wherever failure or disaster looms, creative minds step up.

In the aftermath of Katrina and Ida, ordinary people found solutions when governments were paralyzed. The collective talent in communities is impressive. No matter what skills and talents are needed, they can be found among the ordinary people, when there's good reason for it. Kudos go to them.

Mardi Gras Throws

Almost anything can be thrown to parade goers. I once caught a baloney sandwich. When the crew runs out of throws, they will toss just about anything to pleading raised hands. The Irish and Italian parades throw cabbage, onions and carrots. How cool is that? You can go home and fix a pot of soup, when the traffic clears. The plastic poop is really in bad taste, but the vegetables are always fresh and tasty.

Going to a parade is not a spectator sport, the object is to get the throw before someone else does. That can mean out catching your competitor or grabbing it off the ground first. Once you have more than you can carry home, you face the challenge of deciding what you are going to do with thirty pounds of throws. It sounds silly, but it really is a lot of fun. It is amazing to watch the lengths people will go to get a solitary throw. A long time ago I found out.

As a young man, I always took my children to parades. I'll never forget the experience of waiting for a parade with three very young antsy sons. There is nothing to do, but enter in conversation with near-by parade goers. I happened to notice a seventy-two year old women seated on a wheel chair. I know she was seventy-two, because she told me so. She also told me she had painful arthritis. She was from Tennessee and had never seen a Mardi Gras parade. I thought it would be nice to give her anything I caught. That was a wasted thought. The bands arrived and she abandoned her safe perch and yelled for throws. It was a miracle! She jumped up and down like a school girl. It was greater miracle when I convinced a parade goer to return my pipe.

I was jumping and diving for throws and my pipe fell out of my pocket. I reached to retrieve it, but a quicker hand got it first. The fast one was none other than my new Tennessee acquaintance. It took me five minutes to convince her that my pipe was not a throw. She relinquished it when I said, "Some crazy stuff is thrown, but nobody would throw a nasty used pipe". Or would they?

Smells

A picture is worth a thousand words, but a smell can unleash a score of pictures. It's uncanny how a smell can summon memories from the tomb of forgetfulness. Smells can be as pleasant as a spring rain or a summer flower, but as nauseating as chicken feathers in hot-plucking water. I remember plucking chickens as a child, but I'd rather not. But I still remember it every time I smell chickens. I bet there are many people who don't mind that smell, and some maybe even like it.

Some people give up cigarettes and switch to pipe smoking, often for health concerns. I switched because I liked the aroma of tobacco. Pipe aroma is pleasant to some, but others dread it. When I smoke my pipe, most people keep their distance, even after my morning shower. There's a curious claim that smokers are less likely to get Covid. If it is true, it is because people keep a distance from smokers. On the other hand, several times I was stalked by people wishing to get a whiff of my pipe. "That pipe reminds me of my dad" (or paw), they would say to justify their behavior. The most positive response I got from my pipe happened on a fishing trip.

I was standing on the boat dock waiting for number four son to park the trailer. Two ladies had just tied up on the adjacent dock. The boat driver, a lady in her fifties, took note of my pipe and told me that her pappy had smoked a pipe. She spoke of her fond memories of him and how I reminded her of him. Then, she got out of her boat, walked up to me on the dock and asked permission to hug me. I gave her permission, and she hugged the stuffings out of me.

Consoling the Anxious

How should one allay the fears and anxiety of the fearful? Some time ago, a friend was facing a serious medical problem. The placement of stints is common today, but just knowing that doesn't remove the apprehension. Sensing the elevated fear, friends of the fearful one try their best to reassure that everything will be okay. It's a nice gesture of friendship, but I don't think it is effective. The very fact that a covey of friends express their best wishes signals the seriousness of the situation. It seems to me that it can have the opposite effect, confirming the seriousness of the matter. What would happen if the opposite approach were used, namely, overstate the seriousness?

As I saw my friend sink deeper into apprehension, I thought I would take a different approach. Of course, that's a self-serving statement. In reality, I need no moral imperative to seduce others into laughing. "Ron, I know that you face surgery tomorrow to implant stints. Listen, I am sure everything will be fine. But in the event that things don't work out. I really do like your Rolex. It's a really nice watch."

His reaction was immediate, as he exploded into laughter. "That's wrong", he declared as his face gave lie to his words. Were I a genius, I would claim that I skillfully engineered a dramatic mood change. But the truth is that I have never claimed to be a genius. I have claimed part-time genius status only. The irony here is that I can't wear watches, and the ones I do own are wasting away, frozen by my magnetism and lost in forgotten places. My motivation was simply this, anything for a cheap laugh. The fact is that my friend came down with mental health.

Why Worry?

D espite the biblical injunction on anxiety, "Do not be afraid," we still worry about so many things. How is it that in the throes of anxiety, we never ask ourselves, "What is the risk of the worst thing happening"? Whatever it is that prompts worry, the risk is lower than being stampeded by rogue elephants. No matter what we tell ourselves, we just can't kick the worry habit. Fortunately for the reader, I am about to give away one of my best kept secrets and a sure remedy for the problem.

Once you realize that you cannot reason your way out of needless worry, you are ready for action. Pay others to worry for you! It's so simple, you are probably wondering why you didn't think of it. Don't beat yourself up, unlike me, you are not a part-time genius. Sounds good, but does it work and how expensive is it? Let me tackle the first question first and then I'll hone in on the expenses involved.

When you complain to friends that you are troubled by the gout, what do your friends do? They try to console you and help you find a remedy. In short, you have other people worrying about your problem. Now, extend the invitation to worry with you to all your friends and family members, you will have a multitude worrying with you. Don't you see, the cure is in the dynamics of relationships? You will feel better just knowing so many care; and someone just might come up with a solution for your gout. But, be careful that you don't turn into a real bore or people will avoid you. You must give people an incentive to worry in your stead.

Many years ago, I suggested to a dear friend that he and I should launch an enterprise that renders a much-needed service, an organization of professional worriers. My friend declined and I was too worried about something to pursue it further. It is such a great idea; I invite the reader to think about the possibilities. Develop a business model to include recruitment and hire of professional worriers. I suggest that a reputable employee search engine be used. The pitch should be, "Why worry for free? We pay top dollar for skilled empathic worriers". Of course, it would be necessary to weed out the untalented. When enough professional worriers are assembled, start your advertisement.

Keep in mind that worriers are a diverse group. your ads must be targeted at the sub-population you want to reach. Some worriers are frivolous and often neurotic. Some have serious problems for which there are no easy solutions. I would recommend targeting the former. Encourage them to rate their problem on the ten-point scale used to rate pain. On the basis of this self-assessment, allocate your professional worriers accordingly. Also, charge no more than fifty percent of the going rate therapists charge.

The benefits of following my suggestions are two-fold. Firstly, you could make a fortune. More importantly, considering the time and effort required to launch a business, you won't have time to worry. This is a golden opportunity. I am sure that within days of reading this snippet, several worry companies will be launched. Why should it not be you? If you decide not to, try a prayer chain; it is free.

Good News

There is a moment in everybody's life when bad news comes. We don't need to look for it. It just happens. Acceptance usually follows initial denial for some. Others may struggle their entire life away and mark the days until death robs them of their pain. Good news is a bit more complicated. Sometimes it hides when we search for it and we often look in all the wrong places. Will we recognize it when we see it?

When I was a child and saw my brothers and sister leave for school, I couldn't wait untill I was old enough to follow. When I finally made my debut, it wasn't long before I longed to be old enough to play in the older children's play yard. Later, I longed to be in highschool. Then, I thought of adulthood and independence. That's where it's at. Like so many before me and so many after me, I reckoned that real life begins in retirement. I don't remember when I realized that good news is not found in the future. In all likelihood, it was a gradual accumulation of life's moments.

One particular incident stands out as particularly instructive. I was simultaneously trying to put three little boys to bed and working on a research paper. At the base of the stairs, with one eye on my papers and graphs and the other preventing illegal descent, I was overseeing bedtime. The children were talking and laughing and miles away from sleep. I was frustrated that their foolishness kept me from doing important work. It was only later when sleep forced me to put away my work did my frustration evaporate. Before all thoughts were dispelled by sleep, a solitary conviction dominated my mind. There is no more important work than caring for children. However, it only took another annoying incident the following day for me to ignore my own insight. And in all honesty, I am still proned to see happiness as a future event. Summoning snippets helps me to realize that it is not.

Appendix A - Poems

As G.K. Chesterton remarked, "If something is worth doing, it's worth doing badly". For grandchildren who are inclined to have big heads, have them read, "Chickens".

Chickens

Chickens fly and chickens walk.
But they can't do it in the dark.

Chickens peck and chickens scratch.
But can't open a lock or latch.

You can put on shoes and a hat.
But even big chickens can't do that.

You can slide and swing on swings.
Chickens can't do those things.

You can move your hands and legs.
Try and try, you can't lay eggs.

Bad Chickens

For grandchildren who need to know that there are consequences for bad behavior, have them read "Bad Chickens" and "Bad Pig".

Bad Chickens

Bad chickens ate my fishing worms.
They may get real bad germs.
If they do, it serves them right.
I think I'll have fried chicken tonight.

A Bad Pig

I once had a pig
That ate my last fig.
"Don't worry", I said.
I'll eat bacon instead.

Brenda

Brenda was written to reproach teenagers enamored with the bad lyrics of contemporary songs by demonstrating to them that any dummy can write bad lyrics.

Brenda

Oh, Brenda caught her finger in the blender.
Brenda caught her finger in the blender.
Brenda caught her finger in the blender.
But the doctor couldn't mend her.

Here comes ole nine-finger Brenda.
Here comes ole nine-finger Brenda.
Number ten is in the blender.

Brenda thought her mate was tried and true.
But he stepped out on her a time or two.
Now when she caught them harmonizing,
Ole Brenda osterized them.

Oh, Brenda caught her finger in the blender.
Brenda caught her finger in the blender.
But the doctor couldn't mend her.

Appendix B – New Orleans' Popular Culture

Every memory is attached to a particular place, its sights, sounds, and smells. Growing up the only world I knew was a typical New Orleans neighborhood. Of course, every place is special for somebody, but New Orleans is known worldwide as a special place. I am told that some people are unaware that New Orleans is in Louisiana, a place name that usually evokes empty stares from foreigners. Talented writers have probed the nature of the city's singularity beyond the tired descriptions found in travel guides. In a sense, every "snippet" is my feeble attempt to capture both the uniqueness and the universality of the New Orleans experience. Arguably, the best description of the City is from a non-native who became an adopted son.

Walker Percy's "New Orleans Mon Amour" depicts a city of contrasts and paradoxes, if not contradictions. It is certainly true that this bend in the Mississippi was home to more nuns and naked ladies than any other place in the world. Black and white, rich and poor, French and American, indigenous Indians tribes, and a host of other immigrants lived together, not in harmony, but with a sense of collective identity, and in time became parties to the work of building a popular culture.

It's known as the "Big Easy" and the "City That Care Forgot", but neither name captures her contradictions and disharmony. Perhaps, the "Impossible City" is an appropriate name, for in truth there should be no New Orleans.

Despite the introduction of canals and the use of electric pumps to drain the land, there still are more mosquitoes, snakes, and alligators than people. The whole of the City is surrounded by water. The isle of New Orleans is bounded by Lake Ponchartrain, the Mississippi, and swamps and marshes. Largely at or below sea level, the alluvial ridges, deposited by the Mississippi and along other streams, are the only land high enough to be dry most of the time. The alluvial soils are rich and capable of producing a variety of agricultural crops. The swamps and marshes support abundant marine life with a diversity to satisfy even the most fastidious palate. But to enjoy the riches of the land and water, one must endure the City's subtropical climate, which except for a brief period in the fall, is unbearably humid.

The French chose to establish a settlement on the east bank of the Mississippi where a ridge of high ground intersects the alluvial ridge, the driest piece of real estate you encounter sailing up the Mississippi. How do you entice settlers from across the Atlantic? You advertise, or to be blunter, you lie.

In the 18th century, before land was cleared and streets constructed, brochures circulated in France and elsewhere, puffing New Orleans and its amenities. Imagine a fully developed city complete with cobblestone streets in a grid pattern and lined with magnificent buildings and caressed by a crystal-clear river. Further picture scores of ocean-going sailing vessels laden with the wealth of nations to be deposited on the already crowded wharves. Now, if you must lie, it is best to make it a big one. Imagine a view of the City on a south to north line. You blink in disbelief as large white sea birds fill the blue sky over the City. Beyond the City is a lush green plain and beyond the plain is the crystal blue lake. In the distance, are majestic snow-capped mountains.

Despite the lack of amenities claimed in her advertisement, by the 1840s New Orleans was well on its way of becoming a premiere American city. Its thriving port attracted northern capitalists and its population dramatically increased to rival many of America's largest cities. By virtues of its size, prosperity, and cosmopolitan reputation, it was one of the few regular tour destinations opera companies made in North America.

It was far more attractive to Yankee, European, and Latin American entrepreneurs than businessmen of the South. Nowhere in the South was there a large population of French speaking freemen of color. Its unique history and development set the stage for its divergence from the more typical Southern city. To be sure New Orleans was and is a Southern city, but with a difference. Linguistically, culturally, and ethnically, it was very unlike the South. In short, it was a Creole Catholic Island in an Anglo-Saxon sea. The mass immigration of both free and slave mulattoes from Hispaniola reinforced Creole language, and culture. The Caribbean element along with the influx of European immigrants from Ireland, Germany, Italy, Russia, and oyster fishermen from the Dalmatian Coast augmented the population of the City. This mixture of people was unlike any other in the South. In the twentieth century, Cubans, Central Americans, Filipinoes and the Vietnamese further diversified the City's population. Despite its diversity, checkered political history, frequent internal squabbles and muddled cultural heritage, it managed to sing songs in affirmation of life. Its music, cuisine, and celebrations, both secular and religious speak of life in all of its wonders.

But diversity is but one necessary cause of the rise of a popular culture. Many American cities are diverse, but remain pluralistic and residentially segregated. In addition to diversity, physical proximity of the subpopulation, competing elites and a seductive worldview are necessary to create a popular culture.

Residentially, most American cities are a mosaic of diverse neighborhoods separated on racial, ethnic, and class lines like the squares on a checkerboard. Historically, old Southern cities were an exception until WWII when suburbanization and other forces altered this pattern.

Prior to the 1950s, New Orleans' neighborhoods were hodgepodges of dwellings of the rich and the poor, black and white, often on the same square block. Of course, there was legal and cultural separation of the races, but that didn't prevent some sense of community across race and class lines. Every neighborhood had its shotguns and doubles; and every neighborhood had at least a few grander homes. To be sure, each neighborhood was a distinct place, but nearly all shared the City's popular culture. New Orleans was a village of villages connected by streetcars.

As a city in a developed economy, even though it was in an economically backward region, New Orleans was not a homogeneous place like most of the small towns and villages all over the world. Small towns, even in developed countries, are parochial with a tendency to be pressure cookers. For some, there is little escape from the boredom and the duties and responsibilities of small-town life. By contrast, large cities provide novelty and freedom. But, life in the big cities can be a vacuum and some individuals feel disconnected and rootless, if not alienated. Between these two extremes, Walker Percy has identified New Orleans as an exception, the best of both social worlds. A popular culture emerges, even in the midst of population diversity and conflict, when all relationships echo community values.

New Orleans' popular culture emerged out of the contention between two cultural elites, Creole French and an American business elite. So irreconcilable were the parties that for a period in the 1830s, the City was politically divided into three municipalities: Americans upriver, Creoles in the French Quarter and immigrants down river from the Quarter. Canal Street was the demilitarized zone separating them and, in the minds of the combatants, its median was neutral ground. Almost everywhere on earth, the strip of land separating the double flow of traffic is called a median; in New Orleans every median is called a neutral ground. Yet, despite the conflict and contention, a popular culture emerged in the City. A constellation of values centered around the affirmation of life proved to be too seductive for the contentious parties to resist. A garden of values became attached to daily rounds of life in public places and blurred the boundary between private and public spheres. No place else was this more apparent than in the churches, both as a physical place in the neighborhood, and as an embodiment of a worldview.

The parish church was much more than a public place of worship, it enclosed and combined the sacred and the secular into a single cloth suitable for people of other faiths and for people who professed no faith. A key to understanding the way in which Catholic faith and piety exerted its influence on the development of a popular culture is to contrast Catholic and Protestant worldviews.

A wide range of prohibited behaviors constricted everyday life in the ninetieth century Protestant South. Drinking, public dancing, gambling, and other behaviors were strictly taboo. These behaviors are sinful, characteristically Catholic, and the faithful were warned of the dangers of Catholicism.

The essential difference in the two world views was their respective approaches to the created world. When creation was completed, God passed judgement without hesitation. Genesis declared, "It is very good". The Catholic worldview highlights the essential goodness of the created world. By contrast, Protestant Reformers were more ambivalent. Wishing to affirm the majesty of God, they feared the ever-present temptation of idolatry. Concern over idolatry is the key difference separating Catholic and Protestant worldviews. The sin of Rome is that she fosters worship of the saints and the Virgin Mary. Intercession through the saints and Mary on behalf of the faithful is equivalent to pagan idolatry, so vehemently condemned by the prophets. Not only does this theological position restructure architecture, removing icons and statues from churches, but it also impacts everyday piety of the faithful. Where are the crucifixes, statues, rosaries, and sacred images among the Protestant faithful? Gone! The bible alone remains as a sacred material object. All the religious art of Christian Europe is banished and its secular counterpart is met with ambivalence. This has a chilling effect on all forms of art, even folk art. No more would there be dancing and singing in the streets in the South, except of course, in New Orleans.

Painting a picture with broad brush strokes conceals important details. Even in New Orleans, the great religions of the world were racially, linguistically and culturally diverse. The Catholic populations included Black and white Creoles, and immigrants from Europe. Irish, German and Sicilian were numerous enough to support separate ethnic enclaves. By the twentieth century, Filipinos, central Americans, Vietnamese and others augmented the Catholic population.

Protestant and Jewish communities were also diverse racially, linguistically and denominationally. Yankee Congregationalists, Presbyterians and Episcopalians coexisted with their co-religionists from the South along with Methodists and Baptists. Blacks could be found in all these denominations and in numerous independent churches.

This diversity among Protestants was mirrored to some extent among the Jews in the City. The early arrival of reform Jews from central Europe were joined later by more conservative Jews from eastern Europe.

People who professed no particular faith found New Orleans' popular culture very appealing. Protestant and Jewish populations, in time, became more accustomed to this "Island of Sin" in the Bible Belt and gradually adopted some aspects of New Orleans' popular culture. Elsewhere southerners could escape life in the pressure cooker by brief short trips to the "Island of Sin". But cultural exchanges work both ways and life in the City was altered, often in subtle ways, by each group domiciled.

Jewish communities reinforced the work of charity in the city both directly through its own outreach and in collaboration with Christians. Community values were supported in a variety of philanthropic efforts in the arts, education and civic life. Protestant churches offered a vibrant example of fellowship to follow by the large congregations of diverse Catholics. No doubt, sound Protestant preaching on authentic faith had a salutary effect on Catholicism in the City.

Native American Indian populations were largely assimilated on both sides of the color divide and are often overlooked. But their legacy remains very much alive in the many place names, and in the traditions of Mardi Gras Indians. No one yawns who views the needle work art continually reintroduced during the Mardi Gras season. The weight and artistry are impressive. The rituals associated with Mardi Gras Indians tie together St. Joseph Day celebration, introduced by Sicilian immigrants, with older elements of Mardi Gras. Cultural differences are borrowed across racial and ethnic lines. Walls that separate become bridges to unite them.

But the popular culture that emerged in New Orleans in the 19th century would have faded precipitously were it not for reinforcement of its values in the secular realm. In the large institutions and small shops, celebration of life became matter of fact in the lives of its people. Significantly, New Orleans' topography played a crucial role in the development of a popular culture.

Dry land is a premium in an area surrounded by water. Canals and the introduction of efficient pumps held the water back. Once drained these previous watery areas were suitable for permanent settlement, but the soil is not stable. But since the soil does not support vertical development, small shotgun houses, with rooms in single file, were built to maximize space. The end result was to set limits on the development of ethnic enclaves. Nowhere in the City were there large ethnic colonies that are common in American cities. Spatial proximity in a pedestrian city increased the opportunity for diverse groups to be neighbors.

From food to music, neighbors tasted the fare of "foreigners". One of the best examples of this sharing is the city's beloved French bread. Many people have noted that the best French bread is baked by German and Italian bakers. And when it comes to music, nothing is more identified with the City than jazz. Drawn from both classical music and the music of the streets, jazz is the best-known product of New Orleans. But what organically unites the many multi-cultural themes and organizes the celebration of life is religion.

Liturgical seasons govern social life cycles as large and small shops anticipate both sacred and secular observances. Beginning with Christmas tide, spiritual and corporeal preparations quicken to a fever pitch as decorations blossom everywhere and gift exchange becomes an obsession. New Orleans echoes worldwide celebrations but continues the party spirit as the Feast of the Epiphany initiates the king cake customs. The cake, with its concealed "baby" and its regal theme imperfectly mirrors the Gospel account of the Magi. These parochial parties serve as preparation for the entire region's celebrations as the carnival season begins. Literally, the word carnival means "throw away the meat" is a call for Lenten penance that begins on Ash Wednesday. But beginning with twelfth night and continuing until Mardi Gras, the carnival season is a time for fun. The parties, balls and parades redirect attention away from the usual cares of work and duty. One is reminded that it is carnival season in a variety of ways, decorations sprout everywhere in the streets on houses, cars, and people. King cakes show up in homes, schools, and workplaces. Then, there are the parades and the crush of crowds slows traffic to a crawl.

Even during lent, New Orleanians manage to transform fast to feast. The Fridays of lent, and in former times all Fridays, call for meatless meals. Fish, crabs, crawfish, shrimp, and oysters are all utilized in a variety of ways to abstain from meat and give new meaning to the Gospel declaration, "my yoke is easy and my burden light". And then there are those respites that make the "burden of lent" more bearable, Saints Joseph and Patrick feast days in mid-March, with their own special foods, customs, and parades.

After Easter celebrations, the liturgy returns to ordinary time as spring turns to summer and the heat and moisture compel escape from nature's oppression. For some, cold beer and hot seafood at the neighborhood tavern is sufficient. For others, lake and gulf breezes, as well as, beer and seafood are necessary. And when heaven claims a notable resident, despite the heat and humidity, there will be a public celebration. Brass marching bands will take to the streets, joined by dancing by-standers, in a community celebration of life.

The first north winds of fall break the spell of summer, if not by September then by October. To be sure, the approach of Halloween is more than a sufficient excuse for parties and get-togethers, but by this time the liturgy draws attention to end times. The first days of November, All Saints and All Souls Days, is a season of reflection, memory, and prayer. We ask our friends in heaven to intercede for us on earth and for the poor souls in purgatory as churches, cemeteries, and florists prepare for the faithful. Family plots are swept clean and adorned with fresh flowers. By December the liturgy is anticipatory, "waiting" for His coming. The light of Christ overcomes the darkness and the end becomes a new beginning. The warp and woof of the liturgy is interwoven with secular celebrations and the celestial and terrestrial form a single cloth. The construction of a popular culture is a scandal to some, a delightful amusement to millions of visitors, and life of the City.

Many American cities can boast of their superior natural beauty, architectural and cultural richness and other notable attributes. Some American cities rival New Orleans' political corruption, crime and filth. But no other American city is filled with folk philosophers, who teach by example, the difference between having and living.